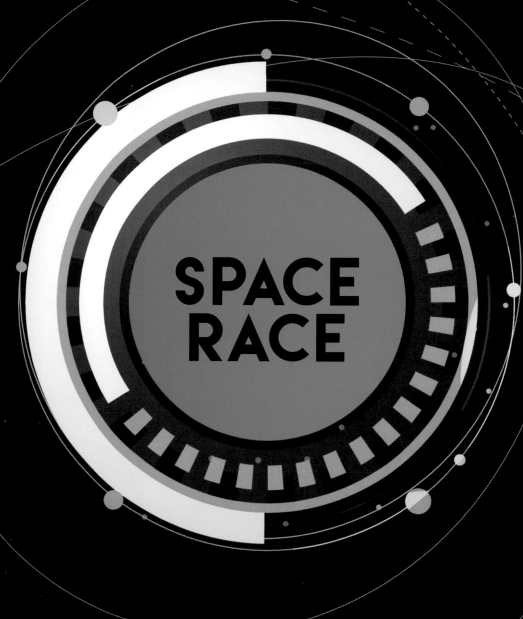

First edition for the United States, its territories and dependencies, and Canada published in 2019 by B.E.S. Publishing Co.

Published in 2018 by Carlton Books Limited, an imprint of the Carlton Publishing Group, 20 Mortimer Street, London W1T 3JW

All inquiries should be addressed to:
B.E.S. Publishing Co.
250 Wireless Boulevard
Hauppauge, New York 11788
www.bes-publishing.com

ISBN: 978-1-4380-5068-3

Library of Congress Control No.: 2018958863

Date of Manufacture: November 2018
Manufactured by: RRD Asia, Dongguan, China

Printed in China
9 8 7 6 5 4 3 2 1

Executive Editor: Joff Brown
Design Manager: Emily Clarke
Design: Ceri Hurst
Production: Nicola Davey
Picture Research: Steve Behan

SPACE
RACE

THE STORY OF SPACE EXPLORATION
TO THE MOON AND BEYOND

BEN HUBBARD

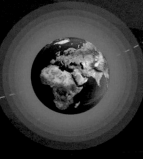

B.E.S.
PUBLISHING

CONTENTS

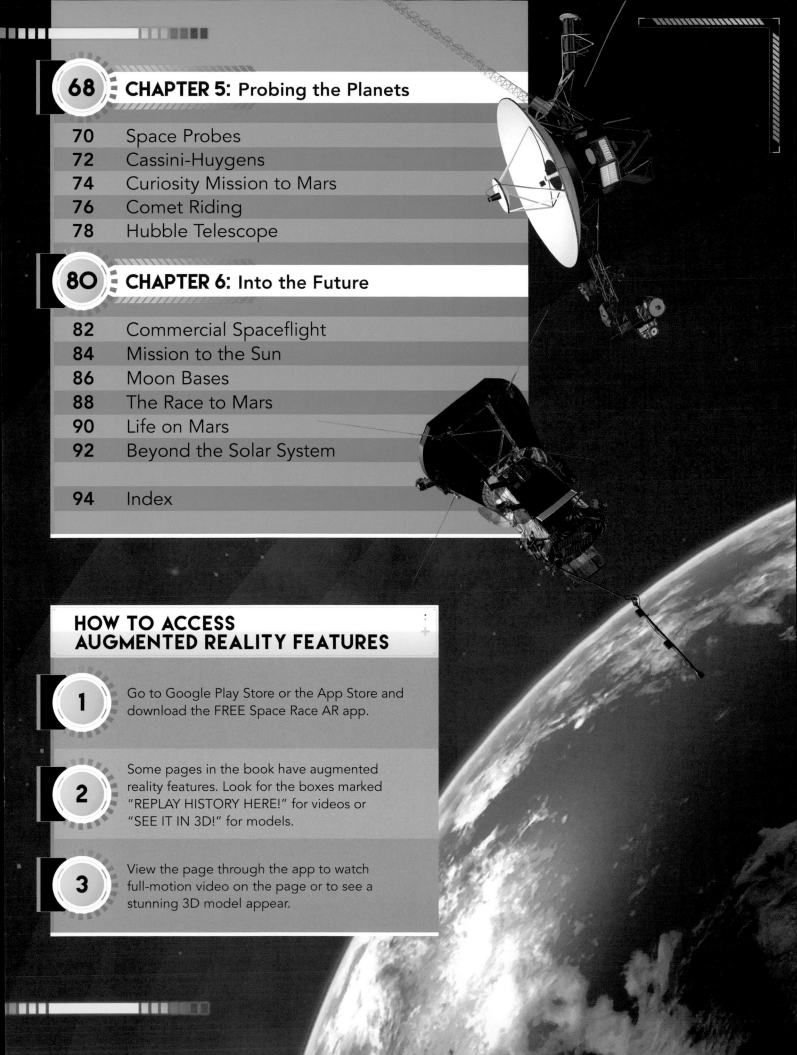

HOW TO ACCESS AUGMENTED REALITY FEATURES

1 Go to Google Play Store or the App Store and download the FREE Space Race AR app.

2 Some pages in the book have augmented reality features. Look for the boxes marked "REPLAY HISTORY HERE!" for videos or "SEE IT IN 3D!" for models.

3 View the page through the app to watch full-motion video on the page or to see a stunning 3D model appear.

1

THE RACE FOR ROCKETS

FOR MANY CENTURIES, SPACE EXPLORATION WAS NO MORE THAN A FANTASY. But in the 20th century, rockets emerged as a means of sending people and objects into space. The first rockets, however, were not created to explore space, but to destroy cities during World War II. Later, two genius scientists would develop this wartime technology in a great competition between the world's two most powerful countries. This became known as the space race.

V-2 MISSILE

DURING WORLD WAR II, THE NAZIS DEVELOPED A ROCKET THAT COULD FLY FOR OVER 200 MILES (300 KM) IN SIX MINUTES AND DROP A BOMB NOISELESSLY ONTO AN ALLIED CITY. This V-2 rocket was a terror weapon constructed with technology years ahead of the rest of the world. As the war ended, the Allies were desperate to get their hands on the V-2 technology.

V-2 ROCKET FACT FILE

LENGTH: 45 ft (14 m)
WEIGHT: 27,500 lb (12,500 kg)
WARHEAD: 2,200 lb (1,000 kg) of explosives
OPERATIONAL RANGE: 200 mi (321 km)
SPEED: 3,580 mph (5,760 kmph)
TOP ALTITUDE: 55 mi (88 km)
FUEL: ethanol/water/liquid oxygen
GUIDANCE: The V-2s were guided by either a radio signal from the ground or a simple computer on board the rocket.

TERROR MISSILE

The Nazi V-2, or "vengeance" rocket, was a missile used to deliberately target civilian areas in the Allies' European cities. Each missile carried a ton of explosives and could reach an altitude of 55 miles (88 km). At this point, the missile's engine would stop and the rocket would drop onto its target at four times the speed of sound. Over 3,000 V-2 rockets were dropped on London and Antwerp during the war.

The V-2 rockets killed about 9,000 civilians in Allied cities. Eyewitnesses said that because the rockets dropped without a sound, the first noise they heard was the explosion.

SLAVE LABOR

Thousands of V-2 rockets were constructed during World War II in a secret factory beneath a hill near the German town of Nordhausen. Slave laborers were forced to construct the rockets. It is estimated over 25,000 of these laborers died, often from illness or starvation.

The Nazi Nordhausen V-2 factory was a death sentence for many thousands of laborers forced to work there.

WERNHER VON BRAUN

Wernher von Braun was a Nazi SS officer and rocket scientist who designed the V-2. He later claimed he was forced to join the Nazi party and never intended to build missiles, but instead rockets that could reach space. When World War II ended, the Soviet and American armies invading Germany sought out the V-2 plans and the scientists who had built them. The Americans had the most success in this when von Braun surrendered himself, his team, and his V-2 plans to them.

Wernher von Braun hid many of his V-2 parts and plans to stop the Nazis destroying them at the end of World War II. He was then taken to America to design rockets there.

SERGEI KOROLEV

Sergei Korolev became the Soviet Union's chief rocket designer after spending six years in a Soviet Gulag, or prison camp. This was the fate of many scientists and intellectuals under the country's communist regime. Korolev was a rocket-science genius who would compete directly with Wernher von Braun during the space race. The two men, however, would never meet.

Sergei Korolev became so important to the Soviet Union's space program that his identity was kept secret for fear the Americans would assassinate him. He was known only as the "Chief Designer."

SPUTNIK SATELLITE

IN 1957, THE SOVIET UNION STUNNED THE WORLD BY LAUNCHING THE FIRST SATELLITE INTO SPACE. The satellite, called Sputnik 1, had been launched on a rocket developed from the Nazi V-2. It showed that the Soviets had superior space technology and was a bitter blow to their American rivals. Now, America would have to play catch-up. The space race had begun.

SPUTNIK 1

Sputnik 1 was a small metal ball with four radio antennae that beeped as it orbited the Earth. The beeps were picked up by radio receivers around the world until Sputnik 1's batteries ran out three weeks later and it fell silent. After 1,400 orbits, Sputnik burned up as it reentered the Earth's atmosphere.

SPUTNIK 1 FACT FILE

DIAMETER: 23 in (58 cm)
WEIGHT: 183 lb (83 kg)
POWER: 1 watt
MISSION DATES:
October 4, 1957–January 4, 1958

LIGHTWEIGHT ALUMINUM OUTER CASING

RADIO TRANSMITTERS

ANTENNAE MOUNT

PRESSURE AND TEMPERATURE SENSORS

ZINC BATTERIES

REAR OF VENTILATION FAN

ORBITS

Once a spacecraft reaches a speed of about 17,400 mph (28,000 kmph), the Earth's gravity can no longer pull it to the ground. However, at this speed gravity still has enough power to keep the spacecraft in its orbit. An orbit is a curved path that goes around the Earth. If the spacecraft maintains its speed in orbit, it will stay there forever.

Premier Khrushchev boasted that Soviet space achievements showed the superiority of the communist political system over the American capitalist system. "Let the capitalist countries try to overtake us," Khrushchev challenged.

Sputnik 2 was much bigger than Sputnik 1. It was 13 feet (4 m) high, and carried sensors and a temperature control system—plus a television camera to transmit images of Laika the dog.

PROPAGANDA PROGRAM

Soviet premier Nikita Khrushchev knew the propaganda value of Sputnik 1 and warned the Americans that more "space firsts" were to follow. Sputnik 1 passed over the United States seven times a day, reminding the Americans of the Soviet success. But more than national pride was at stake. With Sputnik, the Soviets showed they had the technology to build a long-range missile that could reach American shores. Now, the United States needed to prove it could do the same.

SPUTNIK 2

Within a month of Sputnik 1, the Soviet Union trumped its own achievement with the launch of Sputnik 2. This was a larger satellite that carried a passenger: Laika the dog. Laika was a Moscow stray who became the first living creature to go into space. Unfortunately, she only survived for six hours before dying of heat exhaustion.

The inside of Sputnik 2 was cramped, but had enough room for Laika to lie down. She was strapped into the pressurized cabin two days before the launch and wore diapers to collect her mess.

AMERICA RESPONDS

AFTER THE SOVIET UNION'S LAUNCH OF SPUTNIK 1, AMERICA RACED TO SEND ITS OWN SATELLITE INTO SPACE. It was announced that the Vanguard 1A satellite would be launched on December 6, 1958. To witness the event, journalists gathered at the Cape Canaveral launch site and millions tuned in on their TV sets. As the countdown began, America held its breath.

3, 2, 1…LIFTOFF!

The Vanguard rocket began lifting off as flames and smoke billowed from its engines. But after rising 3 feet (1 m), the rocket lost power and fell back onto its launch pad. Then, an explosion tore through the rocket and it toppled over. As it fell forward, the satellite fell from the top of the rocket, rolled along the ground, and began beeping. The launch had been a complete disaster.

REPLAY HISTORY HERE!

FLOPNIK

The failed launch of the Vanguard satellite was a great humiliation for the American government. It had always promoted itself as a world leader in science and technology. Now it had failed to match the space achievement of its great rival, the Soviet Union. American newspapers wrote damning headlines using wordplays on the name Sputnik to describe the failed launch. These included "Kaputnik," "Oopsnik," and "Flopnik."

EXPLORER 1

The Vanguard 1A Satellite had been launched by the US Navy, but after its failure, the American government turned to Wernher von Braun. Von Braun said he could launch a satellite called Explorer 1 into space within ninety days. On January 31, 1958, Explorer 1 was successfully launched into space. Von Braun had been true to his word, but America was still behind in the space race.

Wernher von Braun

TEMPERATURE SENSORS

NOSE CONE

METEOR PARTICLE DETECTION SENSOR

ANTENNA WIRE

SPACE SPEAR

Explorer 1 was a javelin-shaped satellite that sat on top of the Juno 1 rocket. The satellite was fitted with a radio transmitter and scientific instruments to record data and send it back to Earth. Explorer 1 transmitted data for four months until its batteries were exhausted.

EXPLORER 1 FACT FILE

LENGTH: 80 in (203 cm)
DIAMETER: 6.2 in (15.9 cm)
WEIGHT: 31 lb (14 kg)
POWER: mercury chemical batteries
ROCKET: Juno 1 RS-29

NEW NASA

In 1958, US President Dwight Eisenhower announced the formation of a civilian—rather than a military—organization to manage the space program. This was named the National Aeronautics and Space Agency (NASA), and it has been responsible for American space exploration ever since.

VOSTOK 1

AFTER THE SUCCESS OF ITS SPUTNIK MISSIONS, THE SOVIET UNION'S NEXT GOAL WAS TO PUT A MAN IN SPACE. To achieve this, Chief Designer Sergei Korolev built the Vostok 1 spacecraft. Vostok 1 was a human-sized capsule that sat above an R-7 rocket. Manning the spacecraft would be cosmonaut Yuri Gagarin.

DESCENT AND INSTRUMENT MODULES

The Vostok 1 spacecraft was made up of two parts: a descent module and an instrument module. The instrument module contained the retrorockets that would fire to slow Vostok 1 down. This would bring the spacecraft out of Earth's orbit and down toward the ground.

INSTRUMENT MODULE

Yuri Gagarin
aboard Vostok 1

YURI GAGARIN

Yuri Gagarin was a fighter pilot who had been selected to train as a cosmonaut for the Soviet Union's top-secret space program. Once on the program, Gagarin competed with several other cosmonauts to become the first man in space. He won the competition because Sergei Korolev said Gagarin's smile and charm would make him a likable celebrity.

RETROROCKETS

OXYGEN AND NITROGEN BOTTLES

COMMUNICATIONS ANTENNA

TILTING TARGET

Vostok 1 was weighted so it would tilt in the right direction to reenter the Earth's atmosphere. However, this could not be guaranteed, so the spacecraft had to be protected with a heat shield on all sides. Its spherical shape helped with this feature.

THE CONTROL PANEL

Vostok 1 had a simpler control panel than the MiG fighter jets Yuri Gagarin had flown. This was because Vostok 1 was fully automated and the pilot could only take control by entering a secret three-digit number into a keypad. The number would only be radioed to Gagarin if he was judged to be sane. This was because the Soviet scientists thought weightlessness might drive a person insane.

COMMAND CONTROL ANTENNA

TV CAMERA

HEAT SHIELD

ACCESS HATCH

DESCENT MODULE

SPACECRAFT INTERIOR

Vostok 1's descent module was so small that there was only room for a control panel and a cosmonaut sitting in an ejector seat. Explosive bolts would blow the hatch off the descent module so the ejector seat, with parachute attached, could exit the module.

VOSTOK 1 FACT FILE

CREW: 1
LENGTH: 15 ft (4.5 m)
DIAMETER: 8 ft (2.43 m)
WEIGHT AT LAUNCH: 10,500 lb (4,730 kg)
WEIGHT AT LANDING: 5,400 lb (2,460 kg)
FUEL: nitrous oxide/amine

VOSTOK 1 (cont'd)

VOSTOK 1 WAS DESIGNED TO BLAST YURI GAGARIN INTO SPACE, MAKE ONE ORBIT AROUND THE EARTH, AND THEN PARACHUTE THE COSMONAUT AND SPACECRAFT SAFELY BACK ONTO SOVIET SOIL. It was the most ambitious and dangerous space mission yet attempted. For the first time in the space race, human life was at stake. On April 12, 1961, Gagarin and Vostok 1 were ready for takeoff.

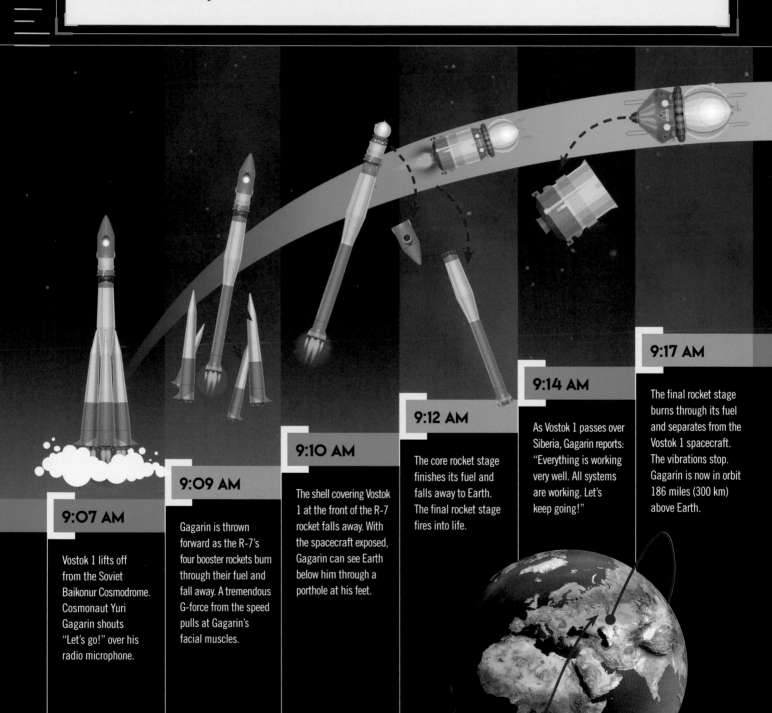

9:07 AM

Vostok 1 lifts off from the Soviet Baikonur Cosmodrome. Cosmonaut Yuri Gagarin shouts "Let's go!" over his radio microphone.

9:09 AM

Gagarin is thrown forward as the R-7's four booster rockets burn through their fuel and fall away. A tremendous G-force from the speed pulls at Gagarin's facial muscles.

9:10 AM

The shell covering Vostok 1 at the front of the R-7 rocket falls away. With the spacecraft exposed, Gagarin can see Earth below him through a porthole at his feet.

9:12 AM

The core rocket stage finishes its fuel and falls away to Earth. The final rocket stage fires into life.

9:14 AM

As Vostok 1 passes over Siberia, Gagarin reports: "Everything is working very well. All systems are working. Let's keep going!"

9:17 AM

The final rocket stage burns through its fuel and separates from the Vostok 1 spacecraft. The vibrations stop. Gagarin is now in orbit 186 miles (300 km) above Earth.

THE R-7 ROCKET

To reach the 17,000 mph (28,000 kmph) needed to break into space, Vostok 1 would harness the power of an R-7 rocket. The R-7 was made up of three rockets, called stages. As each stage finished its fuel, it would fall away. Finally, only the small Vostok spacecraft at the top would be left to orbit Earth.

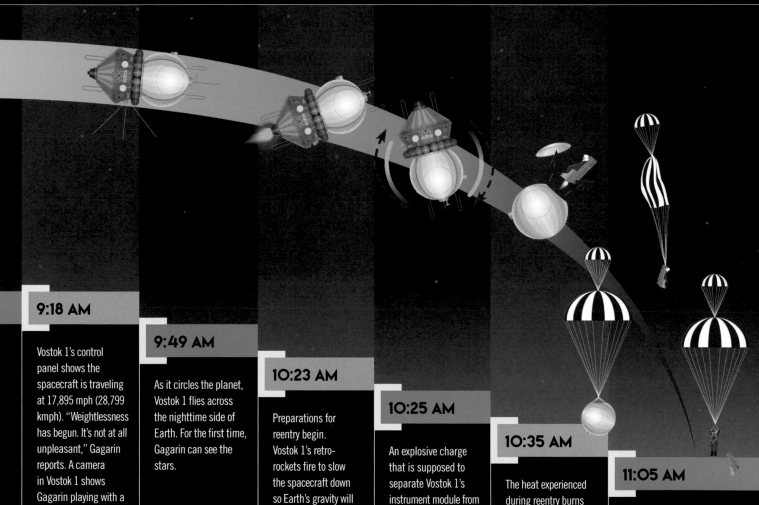

9:18 AM

Vostok 1's control panel shows the spacecraft is traveling at 17,895 mph (28,799 kmph). "Weightlessness has begun. It's not at all unpleasant," Gagarin reports. A camera in Vostok 1 shows Gagarin playing with a weightless globule of water.

9:49 AM

As it circles the planet, Vostok 1 flies across the nighttime side of Earth. For the first time, Gagarin can see the stars.

10:23 AM

Preparations for reentry begin. Vostok 1's retro-rockets fire to slow the spacecraft down so Earth's gravity will pull it out of orbit.

10:25 AM

An explosive charge that is supposed to separate Vostok 1's instrument module from its descent module fails. The spacecraft goes into a spin as it falls toward Earth.

10:35 AM

The heat experienced during reentry burns through the wires holding together the instrument module and descent module. Gagarin ejects and both he and the spacecraft parachute to Earth separately.

11:05 AM

Gagarin lands in a field in Siberia near a farmer's wife and her daughter. "Don't be afraid, I am a Soviet like you!" he tells them, and explains that he has descended from space and needs to find a telephone to call Moscow. Gagarin has only been in space for 108 minutes, but it will make him an international celebrity for life.

HUMANS IN SPACE

DURING THE 1950s, THE SOVIET UNION HAD SHOWN ITS DOMINANCE IN THE SPACE RACE WITH AMERICA. Now, as the 1960s dawned, America announced its most ambitious space project to date. It would attempt to put a man on the Moon by the end of the decade. The Soviet Union would do everything in its power to beat America in this goal. Whichever nation succeeded first would win the space race and prove itself the greatest technological power in the world.

MERCURY MISSIONS

AFTER YURI GAGARIN BECAME THE FIRST MAN TO GO INTO SPACE IN 1961, AMERICA WAS DESPERATE TO SETTLE THE SCORE. The newly formed NASA announced a series of manned missions to space aboard its new Mercury spacecraft. The astronauts undertaking these flights became known as the Mercury Seven.

FREEDOM 7

On May 5, 1961, NASA launched the Mercury spacecraft Freedom 7 with astronaut Alan Shepard aboard. This made Shepard the first American in space. However, the mission's Mercury-Redstone rocket was not powerful enough to put the spacecraft into the Earth's orbit. Therefore, Freedom 7 only spent 15 minutes in suborbital space before splashing back down into the Atlantic Ocean.

The silver suits designed for the Mercury Seven astronauts became a lasting image of the first American missions into space.

FRIENDSHIP 7

Following the success of Freedom 7, NASA launched its first mission into the Earth's orbit. On February 20, 1962, astronaut John Glenn soared into orbit about 165 miles (265 km) above the Earth aboard spacecraft Friendship 7. However, before splashdown, Friendship's warning sensors indicated its heat shield was loose. Without the shield, the spacecraft would burn up during re-entry. Luckily, this proved to be a false alarm and Glenn returned safely.

John Glenn was picked to be the first astronaut to orbit the Earth for similar reasons to cosmonaut Yuri Gagarin: both were charming, friendly, and modest.

THE MERCURY SPACECRAFT

NASA's Mercury spacecraft were smaller and lighter than the Soviet Vostoks. This was so they could be launched into space aboard the less-powerful American rockets. But unlike Vostok, the Mercury astronauts had a joystick inside their cramped spacecraft to take manual control if they needed to.

MERCURY SPACECRAFT FACT FILE

CREW: 1
LENGTH: 11 ft (3.5 m)
DIAMETER: 6 ft (1.89 m)
WEIGHT AT LAUNCH: 4,263 lb (1,934 kg)
WEIGHT AT LANDING: 2,491 lb (1,130 kg)
ENGINE: rocket retropack

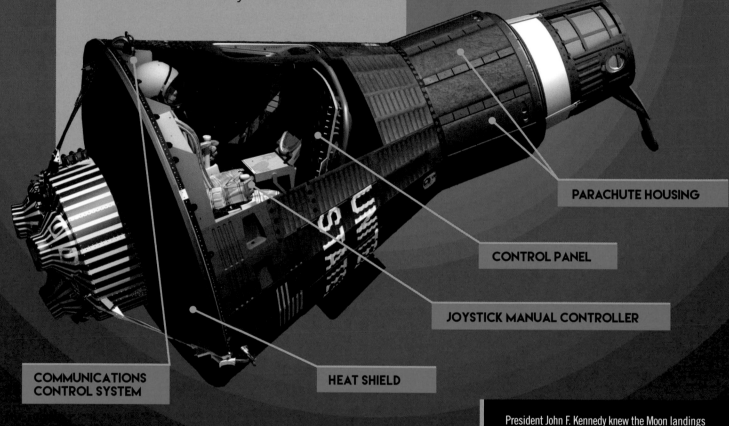

PARACHUTE HOUSING

CONTROL PANEL

JOYSTICK MANUAL CONTROLLER

COMMUNICATIONS CONTROL SYSTEM

HEAT SHIELD

President John F. Kennedy knew the Moon landings would make him popular and restore some national pride after the previous American space race defeats.

KENNEDY CONGRATULATES

Upon his return to Earth, four million people turned out to welcome back John Glenn in New York, and President John F. Kennedy awarded him with a Distinguished Service Medal. Kennedy had shocked the world the year before by announcing America would put a man on the Moon by the end of the 1960s. Upon hearing the news, the Soviet Union resolved to carry out this monumental task first.

SPACE PROBES

WITH THE RACE TO PUT MEN ON THE MOON UNDERWAY, BOTH AMERICA AND THE SOVIET UNION LAUNCHED UNMANNED PROBES TO STUDY ITS SURFACE. Some probes flew by and photographed the Moon, while others crash-landed on it. There were also probes sent out to distant planets in the Solar System.

WHAT IS A PROBE?

A probe is an unmanned spacecraft that travels through space to collect photos and scientific information. The information is then beamed back to Earth for scientists to study. To escape Earth's orbit, a spacecraft must reach a speed of 25,022 mph (40,270 kmph). To make this task easier, early probes were made small and lightweight.

LUNA 1

The Soviet Union's Luna 1 was the first probe to be launched into space in 1959. Luna 1 was supposed to land on the Moon, but it missed its target and instead went into orbit around the Sun. Later that year, the Soviet Luna 3 took the first photographs of the far side of the Moon. Probes to the Moon were important because no one knew what humans might discover when they landed there.

LONG RADIO AERIALS TRANSMIT DATA BACK TO EARTH

TOTAL WEIGHT OF 795 LB (361 KG)

TUBULAR ROD CONTAINS ATMOSPHERE-MEASURING EQUIPMENT

SPHERICAL OUTER CASING PROTECTS INSTRUMENTS INSIDE

LUNA 9

In 1966, the Soviet probe Luna 9 became the first probe to make a controlled landing on the Moon. At the next stage, the probe ejected an egg-shaped capsule containing a camera. When it had taken some photos, Luna 9 beamed them back to Earth using its radio aerials.

PULSED RADAR ALTIMETER

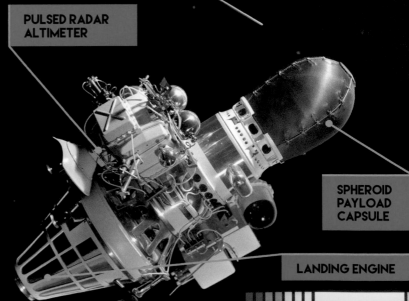

SPHEROID PAYLOAD CAPSULE

LANDING ENGINE

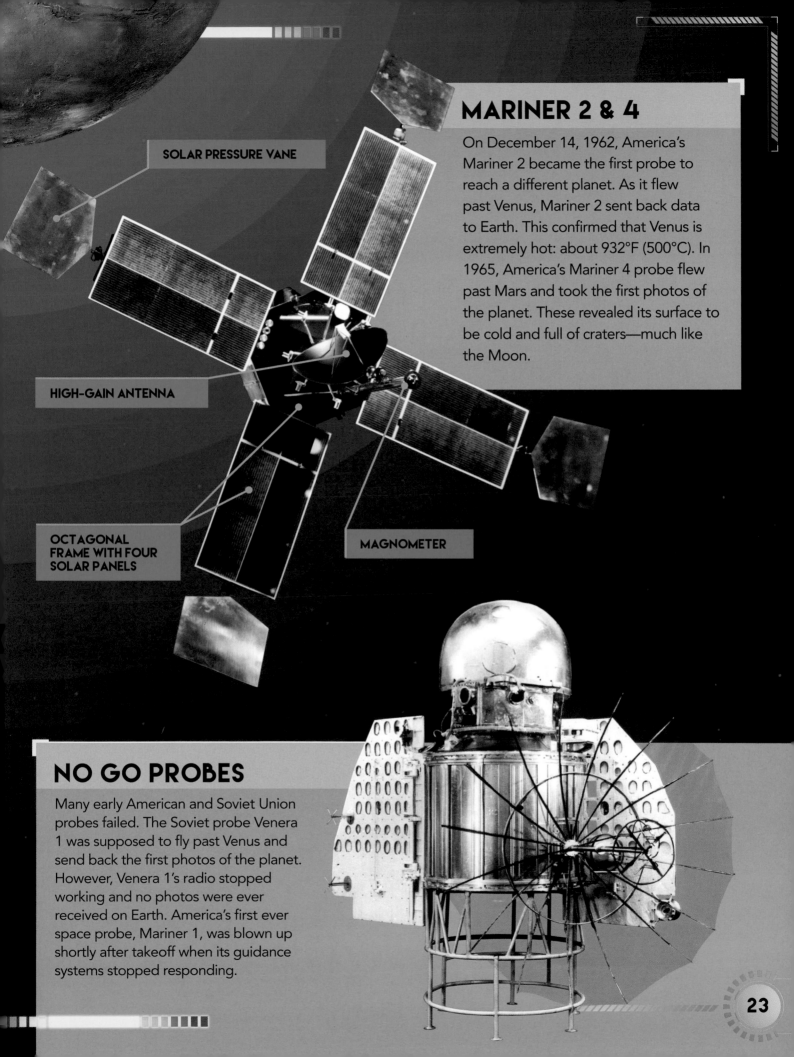

MARINER 2 & 4

On December 14, 1962, America's Mariner 2 became the first probe to reach a different planet. As it flew past Venus, Mariner 2 sent back data to Earth. This confirmed that Venus is extremely hot: about 932°F (500°C). In 1965, America's Mariner 4 probe flew past Mars and took the first photos of the planet. These revealed its surface to be cold and full of craters—much like the Moon.

SOLAR PRESSURE VANE

HIGH-GAIN ANTENNA

OCTAGONAL FRAME WITH FOUR SOLAR PANELS

MAGNOMETER

NO GO PROBES

Many early American and Soviet Union probes failed. The Soviet probe Venera 1 was supposed to fly past Venus and send back the first photos of the planet. However, Venera 1's radio stopped working and no photos were ever received on Earth. America's first ever space probe, Mariner 1, was blown up shortly after takeoff when its guidance systems stopped responding.

VOSKHOD VEHICLES

DURING THE EARLY 1960s, THE SOVIET UNION UNDERTOOK MANY DARING AND AMBITIOUS SPACE "FIRSTS" TO STAY AHEAD OF THE UNITED STATES. These included the first woman in space, the first full-day mission in Earth's orbit, and the first three-man space team. The United States, however, was close behind. When NASA announced its design for a new Gemini spacecraft, the Soviets began taking risks and cutting corners to compete.

COSMONAUT FIRSTS

In August 1961, 25-year-old Soviet cosmonaut Gherman Titov achieved several space firsts aboard his Vostok 2 spacecraft. Titov became the youngest person to visit space, the first to stay in orbit for a whole day, and the first to film the Earth. He also became the first human to vomit in space, after suffering from space sickness.

Titov had been Yuri Gagarin's backup for the Sputnik mission, but like Gagarin, he flew into space only once. Titov was considered difficult and argumentative by his superiors.

FIRST WOMAN

On June 16, 1963, Valentina Tereshkova was launched into Earth's orbit aboard Vostok 6 to become the first woman in space. Tereshkova spent 71 hours in space and orbited the Earth 48 times. She experienced space sickness during the mission but returned unharmed. A woman would not visit space again for another 19 years.

While in space, Tereshkova was reported to be uncommunicative with mission control on the ground. However, she still became a national hero upon her return.

THREE-MAN MISSION

When Chief Designer Sergei Korolev learned America was constructing a new and superior spacecraft called Gemini, he rushed to achieve another Soviet first. This was a three-man mission aboard a new spacecraft called Voskhod. Voskhod was simply an enlarged Vostok with some risky adaptations. For example, there was no room on Voskhod for ejector seats or spacesuits. This meant if anything went wrong, there was no means of escape or any protection from the freezing vacuum of space.

Voskhod was the first spacecraft to carry passengers who were not trained cosmonauts. One of Voskhod's crewmembers was a physician and the other an engineer.

VOSKHOD TAKEOFF

Despite being one of the riskiest missions to date, Voskhod 1 was another Soviet success. Launched on October 12, 1964, Voskhod 1 spent a day in orbit before returning its passengers safely to Earth. Although Voskhod 1 was in reality a hurriedly adapted Vostok, the Soviets told the world it was a brand new, advanced design. Voskhod meant the Soviets kept their lead in the space race.

GEMINI

AMERICA'S GEMINI WAS DESIGNED TO BE THE MOST ADVANCED SPACECRAFT THE WORLD HAD YET SEEN. It was the first spacecraft able to change its orbit and actually fly in space. It also had the capability to dock with other spacecraft. This showed the vast amount of money and resources the United States was investing into the space race, and was a great worry for the underfunded Soviet program.

TAKING FLIGHT

Before Gemini, a spacecraft was simply blasted into space and then followed its launch trajectory, or flight path. But Gemini was constructed with rockets that allowed it to change orbit in space. In many people's eyes, this made it the first real spaceship.

TITAN TAKEOFF

All Gemini spacecraft were launched by a Titan II rocket. Titan was a two-stage rocket with three hypergolic fuel engines. This meant the fuel combusted, or exploded, without using an ignition system. The engines were therefore simpler and more reliable.

Titan II rockets were so successful that modified versions were used for space launches until 2003.

ORBIT CONTROL THRUSTER

HEAT SHIELD

RETROGRADE ROCKET

FLIGHT DECK

Gemini's array of control panels and hand controllers made it look like the flight deck of a fighter jet. Therefore, only trained astronauts were used on the Gemini missions.

CORRUGATIONS TO STRENGTHEN THE SPACECRAFT

REENTRY CONTROL SYSTEM

HELPFUL HATCHES

Gemini's equipment module was fitted with many hatches for access to its machinery and components. This allowed objects like fuel tanks to be easily replaced during testing.

INSTRUMENT PANEL

EJECTOR SEAT

MANEUVER THRUSTER

GEMINI 3 FACT FILE

CREW: 2
Gus Grissom (astronaut)
John Young (astronaut)
LENGTH: 18.4 ft (5.61 m)
DIAMETER: 9.8 ft (3 m)
WEIGHT: 7,134 lb (3,236 kg)

SPACECRAFT SECTIONS

Gemini was made up of three sections: a reentry module, a retrograde section, and an equipment module. The crew sat in the reentry module, while their power and oxygen came from the equipment module. The retrograde section housed the thrusters to change orbits, and the retrorockets for reentry.

NASA
GEMINI

SPACEWALKING

IN 1965, THE SOVIET UNION PERFORMED ITS LAST SPACE SPECTACULAR. While in orbit, cosmonaut Alexei Leonov exited his Voskhod 2 spacecraft and made the first ever spacewalk. Only 15 days later, Gemini 4 astronaut Ed White made the first spacewalk for America. While the world marveled at the spacewalking photos, both missions had faced life-threatening issues behind the scenes.

SOVIET SPACEWALKING

Voskhod 2's mission was to orbit the Earth once and then let out cosmonaut Alexi Leonov through an inflatable airlock. Leonov climbed into the airlock, slid open the spacecraft's hatch, and floated into space. A 16-foot (5-m) cord kept Leonov attached to Voskhod 2. At the start, Leonov was delighted with his 12-minute spacewalk, but things quickly began to go wrong.

BALLOONING PRESSURE

After a few minutes, Leonov's spacesuit began to inflate and balloon out of shape. Leonov could no longer get through Voskhod 2's airlock and he was becoming dangerously overheated in the suit. At the last moment, he was able to deflate some of the air from his suit and squeeze through the airlock.

"What struck me most was the silence.

It was a great silence, unlike any I have encountered on Earth, so vast and deep that I began to hear my own body: my heart beating, my blood vessels pulsing."

Alexi Leonov
remembers his spacewalk

ALARMING REENTRY

Back inside Voskhod 2, Leonov and his co-pilot Pavel Belyayev found the orbital module had not separated from the spacecraft for reentry. As Voskhod 2 plunged toward Earth, it went into a spin that only stopped when the cords attaching the orbital module burned away. The spacecraft landed in a dense Siberian forest, where the cosmonauts had to spend the night in the snow surrounded by wolves and bears.

AMERICAN EFFORTS

Astronaut Ed White experienced problems during his spacewalk from his Gemini 4 spacecraft. White was attached to his craft with a tether and moved himself around in space using a handheld jet gun that sprayed pressurized gas. After 20 minutes, White was called back to Gemini. But once inside he initially could not relatch the hatch. This would have caused the deaths of both astronauts during reentry, had White not finally been able to shut the door. Spacewalking had proved a hazardous task.

The glossy color photos of White's spacewalk (called an Extra Vehicular Activity in America) would amaze the world. During the Soviet spacewalk, Alexei Leonov had been unable to activate his color camera.

"I'm not coming in, this is fun...

I'm coming back in... and it's the saddest moment of my life."

Ed White, after being twice told to reenter his Gemini 4 spacecraft.

3

THE MOON IN VIEW

BY THE MID-1960s, THE SPACE RACE HAD BECOME FAST AND FRANTIC. As America's deadline for sending men to the Moon drew closer, the Soviets desperately tried to outdo their superpower rival. But behind the closed doors of the top-secret Soviet space program, cracks had begun to appear. America also suffered under the strain of its ambitious Moon challenge, which was closely followed by its press and public. Lives from both superpowers would be lost in these decisive years of the space race.

BASES ARE LOADED

THE AMERICAN AND SOVIET APPROACHES TO THEIR SPACE PROGRAMS COULDN'T HAVE BEEN MORE DIFFERENT. From America's space center in Cape Canaveral, Florida, every success and failure was played out in full view of the country's media. The Soviet Union's Baikonur Cosmodrome, by comparison, was so secret that most people did not know where it was located, let alone what went on there.

CAPE CANAVERAL

Cape Canaveral is a sandy spit of land almost entirely surrounded by water that provides a safe spot from which to launch rockets. From its beginning as a missile launch site in 1949, it grew into a major space port which included multiple launch pads, a vehicle assembly building, a space-shuttle landing facility, and an Air Force Station.

BAIKONUR COSMODROME

The Cosmodrome that launched all of the Soviet Union's rockets into space was built in a remote, desert-like region of Kazakhstan. Over time, the Cosmodrome became the world's largest space launch site, although there was nothing on the site when building work secretly began in 1955. Even the name Baikonur was given to the Cosmodrome to keep its location hidden: the real Baikonur was a town situated over 186 miles (300 km) away.

To travel the 2.5 miles (4 km) from its hanger to launch pad, the Soviet rockets were towed along a railway track by a locomotive.

ROCKET BUILDING

To build the massive Saturn V rockets needed to send men to the Moon, one of the largest buildings in the world was constructed at Cape Canaveral. Completed in 1965, the Vehicle Assembly Building stands 525 feet (160 m) tall, covers over 344,445 sq ft (32,000 sq m) of land, and used nearly 112,000 tons (100,000 tonnes) of steel in its construction. Inside, 71 cranes and hoists were used to build the rockets, and 453-foot-tall (138-m) doors allowed them to be rolled out to their launch pads.

Used to transport the rockets 2.85 miles (4.6 km) to their launch pads, the Crawler-Transporter is 20 feet (6 m) high, weighs 3,000 tons (2,720,000 kg), and is one of the largest land vehicles in the world.

PRESS AND PUBLIC

Unlike the Soviet space program, NASA involved the country's media in almost everything it did. This meant there was popular support for the expensive space program among the American public.

The American media were given a prime position for all of NASA's rocket launches. By comparison, only successful Soviet rocket launches were reported by its state-run news agency.

SATURN V

THE US PROJECT TO SEND MEN TO THE MOON WAS NAMED APOLLO, AFTER THE APOLLO SPACECRAFT THAT WOULD FLY THEM THERE. But to launch the spacecraft would require the most powerful rocket ever built. This was the Saturn V: a rocket made up of three smaller rockets called stages. These stages would generate the necessary thrust to fire the Apollo spacecraft out of the Earth's orbit and toward the Moon.

REPLAY HISTORY HERE!

1

STAGE 1
Stage 1 would fire for two and a half minutes to boost the Saturn V to 41.6 miles (67 km) above the Earth, before falling away.

SATURN V FACT FILE

HEIGHT: 363 ft (110.6 m)
DIAMETER: 33 ft (10.1 m)
WEIGHT AT LAUNCH: 6,698,745 lb (3,038,500 kg)
UNFUELED WEIGHT: 404,316 lb (183,395 kg)
ENGINES: rocketdyne F-1/J-2
FUEL: liquid oxygen/liquid hydrogen/ rocket propellant-1 (kerosene)

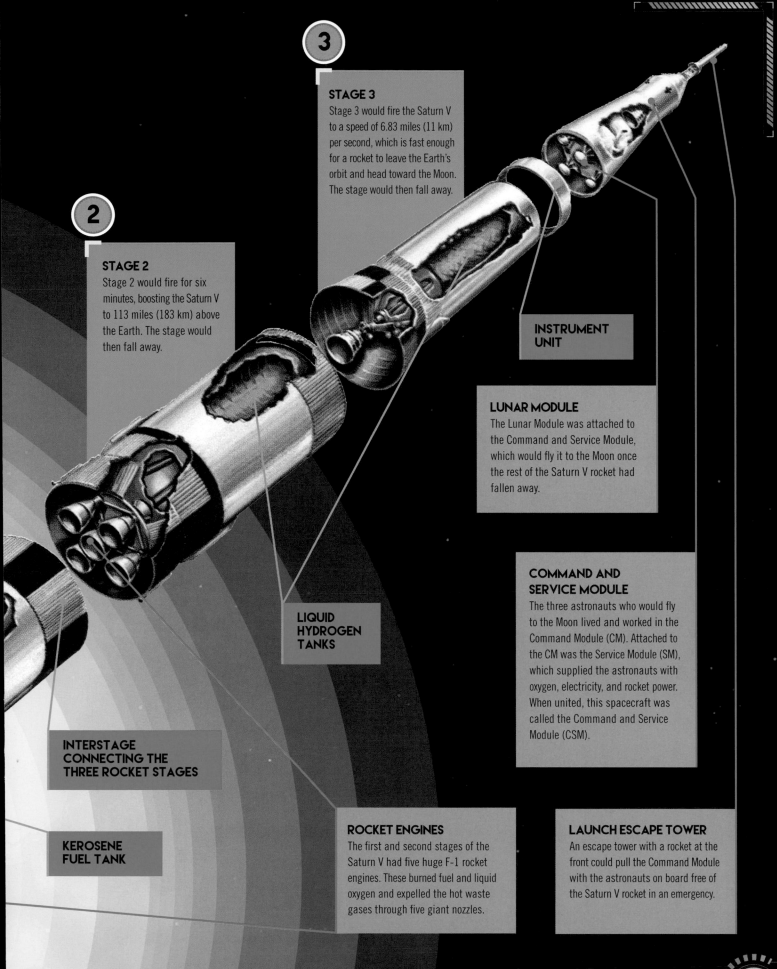

3

STAGE 3
Stage 3 would fire the Saturn V to a speed of 6.83 miles (11 km) per second, which is fast enough for a rocket to leave the Earth's orbit and head toward the Moon. The stage would then fall away.

2

STAGE 2
Stage 2 would fire for six minutes, boosting the Saturn V to 113 miles (183 km) above the Earth. The stage would then fall away.

INSTRUMENT UNIT

LUNAR MODULE
The Lunar Module was attached to the Command and Service Module, which would fly it to the Moon once the rest of the Saturn V rocket had fallen away.

LIQUID HYDROGEN TANKS

COMMAND AND SERVICE MODULE
The three astronauts who would fly to the Moon lived and worked in the Command Module (CM). Attached to the CM was the Service Module (SM), which supplied the astronauts with oxygen, electricity, and rocket power. When united, this spacecraft was called the Command and Service Module (CSM).

INTERSTAGE CONNECTING THE THREE ROCKET STAGES

KEROSENE FUEL TANK

ROCKET ENGINES
The first and second stages of the Saturn V had five huge F-1 rocket engines. These burned fuel and liquid oxygen and expelled the hot waste gases through five giant nozzles.

LAUNCH ESCAPE TOWER
An escape tower with a rocket at the front could pull the Command Module with the astronauts on board free of the Saturn V rocket in an emergency.

APOLLO SPACECRAFT

SITTING ABOVE THE MIGHTY SATURN V ROCKET WAS THE APOLLO SPACECRAFT THAT WOULD TAKE THE THREE AMERICAN ASTRONAUTS TO THE MOON. Apollo was made up of the Command Module, the Service Module, and the Lunar Module, also known as the Eagle. The Command and Service Modules remained united at all times except during reentry to Earth.

LUNAR MODULE

The Lunar Module had two parts: a descent stage with a rocket engine, scientific equipment, and landing legs; and an ascent stage, with a small rocket engine and living quarters for the crew.

LUNAR MODULE FACT FILE

CREW: 2
LENGTH: 22.9 ft (6.98 m)
DIAMETER: 31.1 ft (9.5 m)
WEIGHT AT LAUNCH: 33,200 lb (15,059 kg)
ENGINES: descent and ascent engines

COMMAND MODULE

The Command Module was the most important part of the Apollo spacecraft. The crew stayed in it for most of their voyage to and from the Moon, and it was the only part of the spacecraft to return to Earth.

COMMAND MODULE FACT FILE

CREW: 3
LENGTH: 11.38 ft (3.47 m)
DIAMETER: 12.86 ft (3.92 m)
WEIGHT AT LAUNCH: 13,110 lb (5,947 kg)
ENGINES: reaction control thrusters

SERVICE MODULE

The Service Module provided vital life support systems, including oxygen and electricity, to the crew in the Command Module. It was also fitted with thrusters to fire the spacecraft back to Earth from the Moon.

SERVICE MODULE FACT FILE

LENGTH: 24.8 ft (7.56 m)
DIAMETER: 12.8 ft (3.92 m)
WEIGHT AT LAUNCH: 54,194 lb (24,582 kg)
ENGINES: service propulsion system

LANDING PAD

DOCKING TUNNEL

REACTION CONTROL ROCKETS

FORWARD HEAT SHIELD

FUEL CELLS

SERVICE PROPULSION SYSTEM NOZZLE

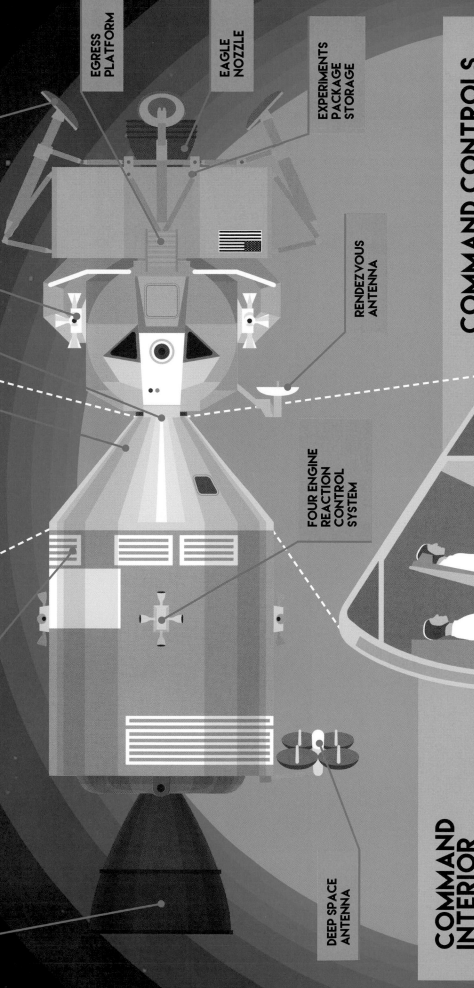

EGRESS PLATFORM

EAGLE NOZZLE

EXPERIMENTS PACKAGE STORAGE

RENDEZVOUS ANTENNA

FOUR ENGINE REACTION CONTROL SYSTEM

DEEP SPACE ANTENNA

COMMAND CONTROLS

Above the astronaut couches in the Command Module was a large dashboard of controls and instruments. Although advanced for its day, the Command Module had about 1,000 times less computing power than a modern mobile phone. To the sides of the control panel were five small windows.

COMMAND INTERIOR

Inside the Command Module were three astronaut couches and a narrow compartment below them for sleeping in zero gravity. Storage compartments around the couches held everything, from toothbrushes and a first aid kit to a map of the stars.

TRAINING FOR SPACE

EARLY SOVIET COSMONAUTS AND AMERICAN ASTRONAUTS HAD TO UNDERGO INTENSIVE TRAINING TO PREPARE FOR THEIR SPACE MISSIONS. Nobody was sure what these men would encounter in space and only the best fighter pilots were chosen for the job. Their space training, however, would be an entirely new experience. It would push the trainees to their physical and mental limits.

ARMSTRONG'S AGONY

American astronaut trainees such as Neil Armstrong were put through a series of tests to prove they had the "right stuff" to go into space. During these tests, Armstrong had to stand in a bucket of ice water while having water squirted into his ear and was then shut in an isolation chamber with no sound or smell for two hours. In another test, Armstrong had to stay in a room where the temperature exceeded 145°F (63°C). He sat still and tried to lower his body temperature to pass the test.

Before becoming an astronaut, Neil Armstrong was a fighter pilot who tested the experimental hypersonic X-15 rocket aircraft.

REPLAY HISTORY HERE!

GAGARIN'S G-SHOCK

Yuri Gagarin's cosmonaut training included being locked in an isolation chamber for 10 days and later having his oxygen reduced until he passed out. Gagarin's most dreaded test, however, was on the centrifuge machine. This spun cosmonauts around at high speeds to imitate the tremendous weight called G-force, which is experienced during liftoff. Most people pass out at 9Gs, but Gagarin was pushed to 12Gs in the centrifuge machine.

The "G" in G-force stands for "gravitational." Humans constantly experience around 1G from the planet's gravity. During a rocket's liftoff, astronauts experience about 3Gs.

VOMIT COMET

On the Moon, there is only one-sixth of the gravity that is on Earth. In space, there is no gravity at all. To imitate the low-gravity conditions on the Moon, astronauts practiced walking in their spacesuits in a swimming pool. To practice being weightless, they trained aboard a reduced-gravity aircraft called the "Vomit Comet." It had this name because weightlessness often made astronauts nauseous.

The Vomit Comet was a converted C-131 aircraft that flew to high altitudes, then dropped into a roller-coaster type free-fall to provide near weightlessness for those inside.

FLYING IN BED

The Flying Bedstead was the name given to a practice model of the Lunar Module that would land on the Moon. Neil Armstrong had to eject from the Bedstead in training when it spun out of control, crashed, and exploded. He was lucky to survive.

The Bedstead's four spindly legs gave the Lunar Module its own nickname: the "Bug."

SPACECRAFT TRAGEDIES

IN ORDER TO MEET THE 1969 DEADLINE TO PUT MEN ON THE MOON, THE AMERICAN APOLLO PROJECT HAD TO BE DEVELOPED AT BREAKNECK SPEED. This meant that equipment wasn't always tested properly and corners were cut. Then, in 1967, tragedy struck when three Apollo astronauts were killed during a routine test. It was later revealed that Soviet space personnel had also died in an accident, although this was kept secret for many years.

TESTING APOLLO

On January 27, 1967 astronauts Ed White, Gus Grissom, and Roger Chaffee were sealed into the Command Module of the Apollo 1 spacecraft to test its equipment. But from the beginning, things went wrong. The communications systems wouldn't work and the astronauts had to stay strapped into their seats for five hours while it was fixed. Then, an exposed piece of wire made a tiny spark and suddenly a fire broke out.

The control room was alerted to the fire by a cry over the radio by Roger Chaffee: *"We've got a fire in the cockpit!"*

TRAGEDY STRIKES

Inside Apollo 1, the flames were fed by high-pressure oxygen and the fire grew quickly out of control. The astronauts tried to unbolt the hatch from inside, but even under normal conditions this took over 90 seconds. By that time, the three astronauts had burned to death. Although NASA came under heavy criticism for the deaths, the Apollo program continued afterward.

In an interview before his death Gus Grisson said: *"If we die, do not mourn for us. This is a risky business we're in and we accept those risks."*

THE NEDELIN CATASTROPHE

The greatest disaster in the history of space exploration took place at the Baikonur Cosmodrome on October 24, 1960. However, it was kept a state secret for many years afterward. The Nedelin Catastrophe occurred during the launch of a test missile. After many problems with the launch, Marshal Mitrofan Nedelin took personal charge and insisted it went ahead. But instead of lifting off, the missile exploded into a massive fireball that incinerated 126 Soviet space personnel, including Nedelin.

Some men trying to escape the flames became stuck fast in a strip of newly laid tar, which melted in the heat.

FAREWELL KOROLEV

In 1966, Chief Soviet Designer Sergei Korolev died suddenly during routine surgery. His body had been weakened so much during his time in the Soviet Gulag that it could not cope with the operation. Korolev's death was a terrible blow to the Soviet space program and all but ended its ambitions to send men to the Moon.

After his death, Korolev's identity was revealed to the world for the first time and he was given a full state funeral. Wernher von Braun would read about his great Soviet rival for the first time in a newspaper.

DESTINATION MOON:
APOLLO 11

ON JULY 16, 1969, APOLLO 11 BLASTED OFF FROM CAPE CANAVERAL. America had met its own deadline to send men to the Moon and beaten its Soviet rivals in the process. However, there were still 234,855 miles (377,962 km) left to travel. Once the Saturn V had discarded its stages, the Command and Service Module would have to transport the Lunar Lander and launch it to the Moon's surface. There was a lot that could go wrong.

LAUNCH ESCAPE TOWER JETTISON
A small rocket on top of the Command Module was designed to carry it to safety if anything went wrong. At this height it was no longer useful and was jettisoned.

STAGE TWO
Stage Two's five rocket engines fired for about 8 minutes. They carried Apollo 11 into Earth's upper atmosphere before separating.

STAGE ONE
Stage One was the most powerful. Its five giant rocket engines carried Apollo 11 to a height of 42 miles (67 km) before falling away into the Atlantic Ocean.

LIFTOFF
It took about 12 minutes for the Saturn V's engines to carry the spacecraft that would travel to the Moon and its three-person crew into orbit around the Earth.

THE SATURN V ROCKET
The 360 foot (110 meter) tall rocket that powered Apollo 11 was made up of three stages. As each stage used up its fuel, it fell away to reduce weight.

STAGE THREE

A burst of Stage Three's single engine carried Apollo 11 up into Earth's orbit. It was fired up again about one and a half orbits later to take Apollo 11 to the Moon.

TRANSPOSITION, DOCKING, AND EXTRACTION

The Command and Service Module (CSM) separates, rotates 180 degrees and docks with the Lunar Module (LM), pulling it away from the Stage Three engine, which is then jettisoned.

INTO LUNAR ORBIT

The CSM and LM form the final spacecraft that makes the three-day journey to the Moon. It then fires its engine for six minutes to slow it down to enter lunar orbit.

LUNAR LANDING

Using a single rocket engine beneath it and smaller steering rockets fixed on its sides, the Lunar Module landed safely on the Moon.

COMMAND SHIP

Columbia remained in orbit around the Moon with just astronaut Michael Collins aboard, relaying signals from the Eagle back to Earth.

THE DESCENT

After 30 orbits of the Moon, the Lunar Module (called Eagle) separated from the Command and Service Module (called Columbia) and fired its descent rockets, carrying Neil Armstrong and Buzz Aldrin down to the Moon's surface.

THE LUNAR MODULE

ON JULY 20, 1969, NEIL ARMSTRONG SEARCHED DESPERATELY FOR A SPOT TO LAND THE LUNAR LANDER ON THE MOON. From Earth, Mission Control warned Armstrong he had only 60 seconds' worth of fuel left. Everyone held their breath. Then, Armstrong's voice crackled over the radio with the news the world was waiting to hear: *"the Eagle has landed."* The astronauts had touched down safely on the Moon.

TWO FOR ONE

The Lunar Module was made up of two distinct sections: a descent stage for landing on the Moon and an ascent stage for returning the crew to lunar orbit.

ASCENT STAGE

This upper section of the Lunar Module was designed to carry two astronauts and housed the flight controls and its own small rocket engine.

DESCENT STAGE

This lower section contained fuel and the descent engine that controlled the Eagle's landing. It also provided a stable platform for launching the ascent stage and was left behind on the Moon's surface when the astronauts returned.

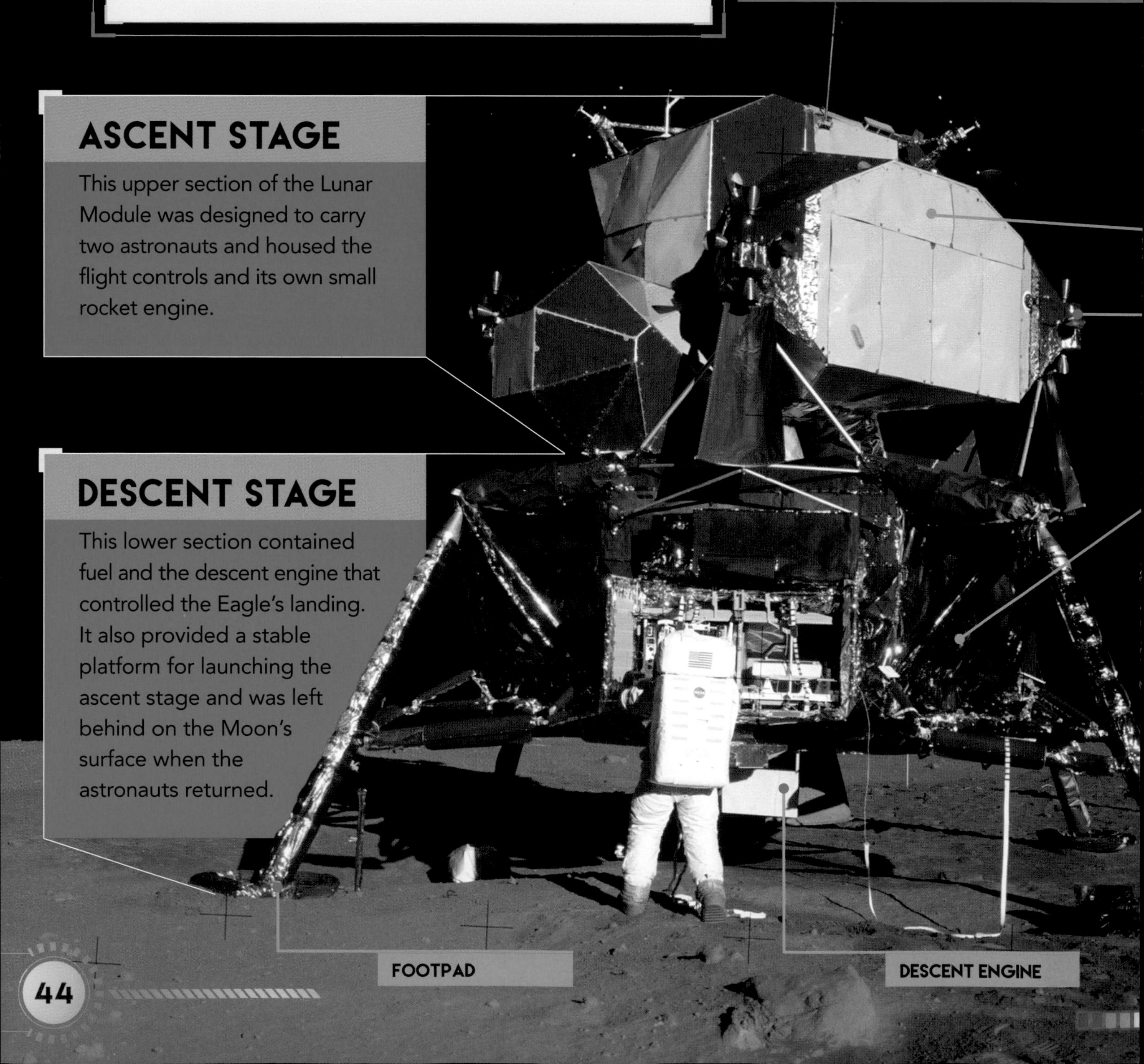

FOOTPAD

DESCENT ENGINE

Neil Armstrong

Buzz Aldrin

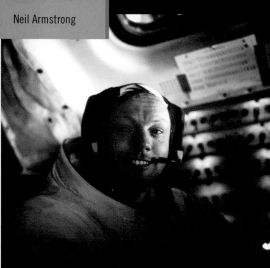

CABIN

The Moon's low gravity meant that no seats were needed in the ascent stage's cabin. The astronauts stood at the flight controls!

REACTION CONTROL THRUSTER

SHIELDING

Specially developed metal alloy and plastic films shielded the descent stage from heat and also from damage by small micrometeoroid particles.

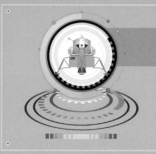

SEE IT IN 3D!

Look at these pages with the Space Race AR app on your smartphone or tablet to see a 3D model of the lunar lander in augmented reality.

APOLLO 11: LUNAR MODULE

CREW: 2 (Neil Armstrong, Buzz Aldrin)
HEIGHT: 22 ft, 11 in (7.0 m)
WIDTH: 31 ft (9.4 m)
WEIGHT (empty): 8,650 lb (3,920 kg)
WEIGHT (with crew and fuel): 32,500 lb (14,700 kg)

MEN ON THE MOON

WHEN THE LUNAR LANDER TOUCHED DOWN ON THE MOON, IT MARKED THE END OF THE SPACE RACE. Wernher von Braun's Apollo design had won it for the Americans. Now, over half a billion TV viewers on Earth were united in admiration as astronaut Neil Armstrong climbed down the Lunar Lander's ladder onto the Moon's surface. *"That's one small step for man,"* Armstrong told the world from his radio microphone, *"and one giant leap for mankind."*

There is no rain or wind on the Moon, so Neil Armstrong's footprint could remain there for millions of years.

Neil Armstrong took most of the Moon photos. He is only seen in one image, reflected in Buzz Aldrin's helmet visor.

LIFELESS WORLD

Apollo 11 astronauts Neil Armstrong and Buzz Aldrin found the Moon to be a cold, lonely place with no sign of life. Its surface was covered with a fine, gray dust that looked and tasted like gunpowder.

MOON TASKS

The first task for the Apollo astronauts was to collect a rock sample in case they had to take off quickly. The sample would give geologists clues about possible signs of water or life on the Moon. The astronauts then unloaded the scientific instruments from the Lunar Lander. These would be used to conduct experiments controlled from Earth, such as measuring "moonquakes" and calculating the Moon's exact distance from Earth.

Armstrong and Aldrin collected over 47.8 lb (21.7 kg) of Moon rock and soil and brought back even more Moon dust that had attached itself to their spacesuits.

CATCHING ON CAMERA

The astronauts took many photographs of their expedition to the Moon and used television cameras to beam footage back to Earth. This allowed the world to see an American flag planted on the Moon, proof of its victory in the space race. The flag had been constructed to look like it was flapping in the wind, although in reality it was still. A plaque and medals were also left on the Moon in honor of the Apollo 1 astronauts and cosmonaut Yuri Gagarin, who had died in a flying accident in 1968.

REPLAY HISTORY HERE!

ASCENT
The Lunar Lander blasts off from the Moon and connects with the CSM.

FLYING HOME

To return to Earth, the Lunar Lander's ascent module blasted off from the Moon and toward the Command and Service Module (CSM). This was commanded by Michael Collins, who stayed in space.

INTO THE CSM
The astronauts transfer to the CSM and the Lander is discarded.

HOMEWARD
The CSM flies to Earth and jettisons the Service Module.

LANDING
The Command Module reenters the Earth's atmosphere and parachutes into the sea.

THE APOLLO SPACESUIT

THE SPACESUIT WORN BY THE APOLLO ASTRONAUTS WAS MORE THAN JUST A PROTECTIVE LAYER OF CLOTHING. It was like a small spacecraft with vital life support systems built in. This allowed the spacesuit to provide oxygen and protection against the extreme temperatures found in the vacuum of space. Without a spacesuit, the astronauts would pass out in seconds and their blood would freeze.

APOLLO A7L SPACESUIT
DATE MADE: 1967
OUTSIDE MATERIAL: shiny Gore-Tex
WEIGHT OF SUIT ON EARTH: 189.5 lb (86 kg)
WEIGHT OF SUIT ON MOON: 30.9 lb (14 kg)
PRIMARY LIFE SUPPORT: 16 hr
BACKUP LIFE SUPPORT: 30 min

HEADGEAR

The Apollo spacesuit's headgear had three parts. The first layer was a tight cap with built-in communications systems. The next layer was a pressure helmet to maintain the astronaut's atmosphere. A final helmet contained a sun shield and visor.

Gold-plated visor shields against sunburn and ultraviolet light

LAYER UP

Underneath his spacesuit, the astronaut had a layer of clothing containing tubes that circulated water around his body to keep him cool inside. To keep warm, aluminum-coated layers went over the top. A urine collection and transfer assembly was worn around the hips to collect urine.

GLOVES

Astronauts wore special "intravehicular" gloves during their time on the Moon. These extra-thick gloves were individually molded to each astronaut's hands and were covered with rubber fingertips to help grip objects.

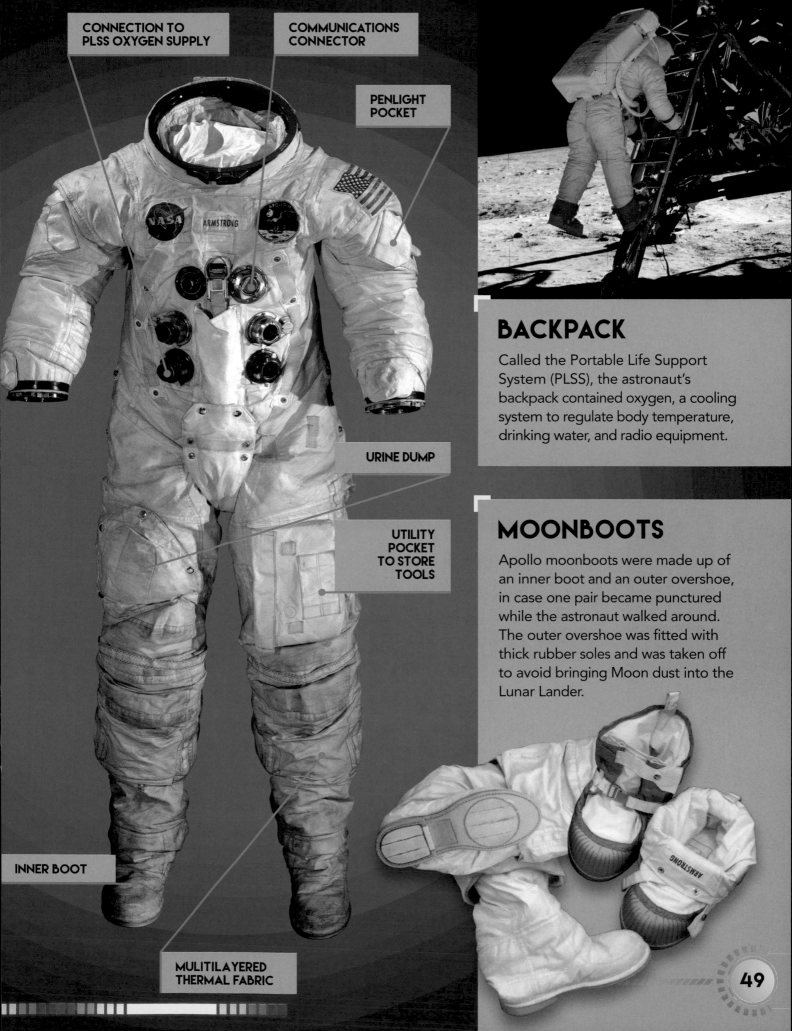

CONNECTION TO PLSS OXYGEN SUPPLY

COMMUNICATIONS CONNECTOR

PENLIGHT POCKET

NASA ARMSTRONG

URINE DUMP

UTILITY POCKET TO STORE TOOLS

INNER BOOT

MULITILAYERED THERMAL FABRIC

BACKPACK

Called the Portable Life Support System (PLSS), the astronaut's backpack contained oxygen, a cooling system to regulate body temperature, drinking water, and radio equipment.

MOONBOOTS

Apollo moonboots were made up of an inner boot and an outer overshoe, in case one pair became punctured while the astronaut walked around. The outer overshoe was fitted with thick rubber soles and was taken off to avoid bringing Moon dust into the Lunar Lander.

4

SPACE STATIONS AND SHUTTLES

AFTER THE SPACE RACE ENDED IN 1969, NOBODY WAS SURE WHAT SPACE CHALLENGE SHOULD COME NEXT. America sent Apollo missions to the Moon until 1972, when the government decided that lunar exploration was too costly. Instead, NASA began to concentrate its efforts closer to home. The agency used the leftover hardware from its Apollo spacecraft to build a more permanent structure in space. The Soviet Union had similar plans. This began the era of cooperative space stations, ending the space hostilities between the two superpowers.

SPECTACULAR SOYUZ

ALTHOUGH HE HAD DIED IN 1966, SOVIET CHIEF DESIGNER SERGEI KOROLEV LEFT A LASTING LEGACY IN THE FORM OF SOYUZ. First launched in 1967, Soyuz was the first Soviet spacecraft that could dock with another craft in space. It was such a successful design that Soyuz spacecraft are still in operation today. Used to transport crew and cargo to and from the International Space Station, it is considered the world's safest and most reliable means of space transport.

SOYUZ FACT FILE

CREW: 3
LENGTH: 8.5 ft (2.6 m)
DIAMETER: 8.92 ft (2.72 m)
SOLAR ARRAY SPAN: 32.4 ft (9.9 m)
WEIGHT AT LAUNCH: 14,462 lb (6,560 kg)
WEIGHT AT LANDING: 6,194 lb (2,810 kg)
FUEL: main engine uses nitric acid/hydrazine; thrusters use hydrogen peroxide

SOYUZ SECTIONS

Soyuz is made up of three modules. While in space, the crew live and work in its front Orbital Module. This module has a hatch connecting it to the bell-shaped Descent Module, the only part of Soyuz that returns to Earth. The Service Module at the end of Soyuz contains the spacecraft's engines and power supply.

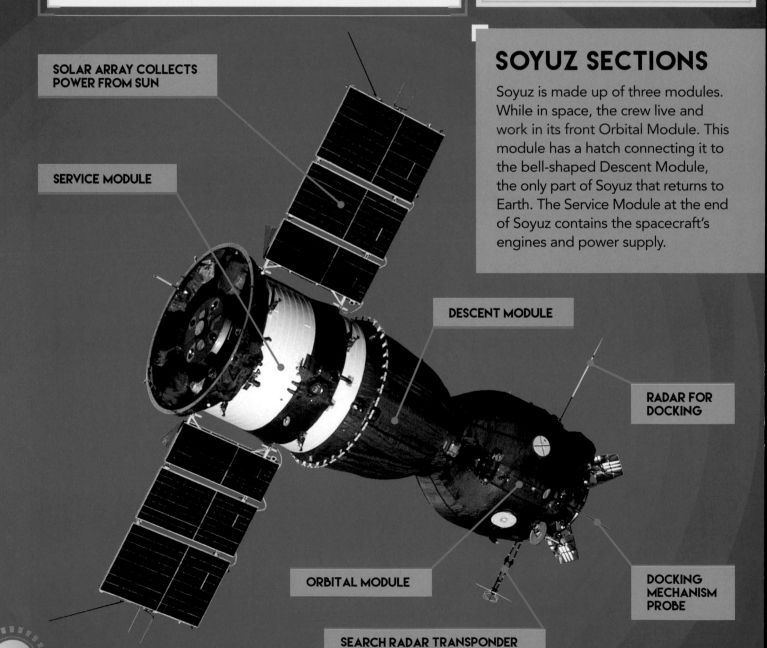

SOLAR ARRAY COLLECTS POWER FROM SUN

SERVICE MODULE

DESCENT MODULE

RADAR FOR DOCKING

ORBITAL MODULE

DOCKING MECHANISM PROBE

SEARCH RADAR TRANSPONDER

SOYUZ ROCKET

Sergei Korolev's spacecraft legacy included not only Soyuz, but also a rocket to launch it. The Soyuz rocket was developed from Korolev's earlier R-7 used to launch Sputnik and Vostok. However, the Soyuz rocket had a new upper stage that gave it more thrusting power.

The Soyuz rocket had three stages. The first and second stages burned away after about five minutes. The third stage burned away about four minutes later, after first boosting the spacecraft into orbit.

SOYUZ-APOLLO HANDSHAKE

In 1975, America and the Soviet Union agreed to end their space rivalry by docking a Soyuz and an Apollo craft in space. This would mean the superpowers could now share their space expertise and come to each other's rescue in space if necessary. On July 17, the Soyuz and Apollo docked and their five crewmembers transferred between the two spacecraft. The mission was like a big handshake between the two superpowers in space.

The crewmembers from America and the Soviet Union had to undergo intensive language courses so they would understand each other in space.

FAREWELL VON BRAUN

Although often haunted by his controversial Nazi past, Wernher von Braun had been the brains behind NASA's Apollo program to the Moon. Von Braun oversaw all of America's Apollo missions, but did not fulfill his dream of a base on the Moon. He died of cancer in 1977.

SPACE STATIONS

AFTER AMERICA LANDED A MAN ON THE MOON, THE SOVIET UNION GAVE UP ON ITS PLANS FOR A LUNAR LANDING. Instead, its space program focused on launching a space station into orbit around Earth. The purpose of the space station was to conduct experiments and see how the human body copes with living in space. The Soviet Union went on to lead the way with space station technology, launching seven Salyut stations between 1971 and 1982.

SALYUT STATIONS

Each Salyut space station had a cylinder shape and three pressurized compartments to house a crew of three cosmonauts. Launched in 1971, Salyut 1 spent 175 days in space and orbited the Earth almost 3,000 times. The crew of Soyuz 11 were the first to live in Salyut 1 and spent 23 days there. However, on their way home, an air valve failed in Soyuz 11's Descent Module and all three cosmonauts were killed.

Salyut was so named in a "salute" to Yuri Gagarin's first manned orbital flight around the Earth.

SALYUT 1 FACT FILE

CREW: 3
LENGTH: 43 ft (13.1 m)
DIAMETER: 13.6 ft (4.15 m)
WEIGHT AT LAUNCH: 41,667 lb (18,900 kg)
FUEL: nitric acid
POWER: 4 solar panels

SENDING SKYLAB

Launched in 1973, America's Skylab was intended to be a ready-made scientific laboratory to conduct experiments in space. Although one of Skylab's solar panels was torn away and its heat shield damaged during its launch, several crews successfully docked and stayed aboard Skylab during its six-year life. Its final crew stayed for a record three months in space, providing important information about the long-term effects of weightlessness on the human body.

The main section of Skylab was built from an empty third stage left over from an unused Saturn V rocket.

SKYLAB FACT FILE

CREW: 3
LENGTH: 118.4 ft (36.1 m)
DIAMETER: 21.6 ft (6.6 m)
WEIGHT AT LAUNCH: 76,000 lb (34,473 kg)
POWER: solar panels

EUROPE'S SPACELAB

Europe's first contribution to space station technology was called Spacelab. A small, reusable station that could fit into the Space Shuttle's cargo bay, Spacelab was designed to carry out experiments in zero gravity. There were 22 Spacelab missions between 1983 and 1998.

SPACELAB FACT FILE

CREW: 6–7
LENGTH: 23 ft (7 m)
DIAMETER: 13 ft (4.1 m)
WEIGHT AT LAUNCH: 28,490 lb (12,923 kg)

Spacelab was an early collaboration between several European countries now known as the European Space Agency.

Skylab

REPLAY HISTORY HERE!

APOLLO TELESCOPE MOUNT

Skylab's primary piece of equipment was the Apollo Telescope Mount: the most powerful solar telescope to be placed into orbit around the Earth. Its job was to take photos and record information about the Sun.

MIR SPACE STATION

LAUNCHED IN 1986, THE SOVIET UNION'S MIR WAS THE LARGEST SPACE STATION YET CONSTRUCTED AND THE FIRST TO BE CONSTANTLY OCCUPIED. Built over a 10-year period, Mir was designed to test whether people could live permanently in space. As such, crews of three stayed on Mir for several months at a time. In 1995, Cosmonaut Valeri Polyakov broke the record for the longest stay in space after living aboard Mir for 437 days.

DOCKING MODULE

In 1995, a docking module was added to Mir so American Space Shuttles could visit. This meant NASA could pay to have its astronauts live on Mir for up to six months at a time. This provided the Soviet Union with some much-needed maintenance money. However, several incidents happened during the American visits to Mir, including a fire breaking out and an unmanned supply ship nearly colliding with the station.

MULTIPLE MODULES

Mir was the first space station to be constructed in space from several different modules. The core module made up the center of the station, but its multiple attachment points allowed six other modules to be added in the course of 10 years. Two of these modules contained docking points and at least one Soyuz spacecraft stayed docked to the station at all times.

CORE MODULE

Mir's core module contained its living quarters and the station's main control console. Because the crew lived in weightless conditions while on board Mir, they moved about the module using handles fitted along its walls. They could stay sitting at the control console by folding their legs under its seats.

MIR SPACE STATION FACT FILE

PERMANENT CREW: 3
LENGTH: 105 ft (32 m)
DIAMETER: 14.27 ft (4.35 m)
TOTAL MASS: 258,392 lb (117,205 kg)
DOCKING PORTS: 2
MODULES: Core, Kvant-1, Kvant-2, Kristall, Spektr, Priroda, Docking Module

KVANT-2 MODULE

Attached to Mir in 1989, the Kvant-2 module contained an area for experiments and instruments and an airlock for spacewalks. Spacewalks were essential to carry out repairs on the outside of Mir. The Kvant-2 module also contained a shower and a system for recycling water from urine. One experiment carried out on Mir was the hatching of quail eggs; the chicks were then raised in space.

SOLAR POWER

Solar panels attached to the Mir module provided the station with its power and charged its batteries for use when the station was in the Earth's shadow. While in darkness, the panels would angle themselves to receive the Sun's rays as soon as Mir moved out of the Earth's shadow.

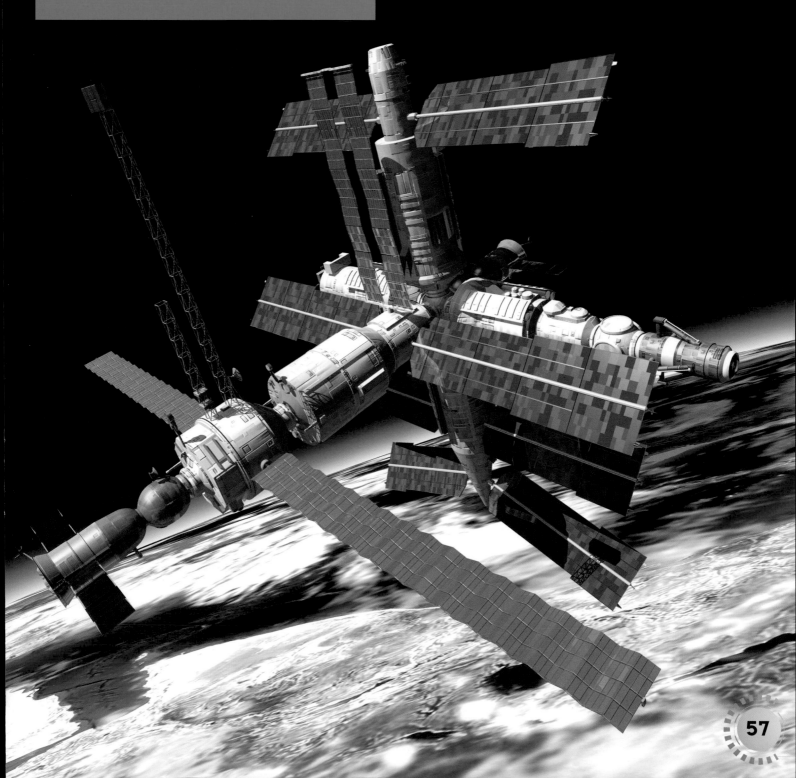

LIVING IN SPACE

LIVING ABOARD A SPACE STATION CAN BE A BIT LIKE BEING STRANDED WITH STRANGERS IN A TINY HOTEL ON A DESERTED ISLAND. However, nothing in space is the same as living on Earth. This is because the weightlessness of space makes even the simplest tasks seem like hard work. Astronauts have to train just to eat, wash, and go to the toilet in space!

Some space station menus include meals such as "Martian bread and green tomato jam."

WORKING WITH WEIGHTLESSNESS

On Earth, human activities include sitting, walking, picking things up, and putting them down again. None of these things are possible in space because weightlessness makes everything float. This means astronauts have to hold on to handles on the space station walls and keep their tools tied to something with straps, or stow them away in a compartment. This can make working in space difficult.

FOOD AND DRINK

All the food on space stations comes specially preprepared and packaged up in vacuum bags or airtight containers. Whole dehydrated meals come in special plastic containers with tubes attached, so water can be added. The meal is then heated in an on board oven. Drinks come served in plastic bottles or as a powder to which water is then added.

Toothpaste tubes in space have their tops attached so they don't float away.

KEEPING CLEAN

There is little water to waste on space stations, and those with showers have to use fans to blow the water toward the bather. Instead of washing with water, astronauts usually get clean by wiping their bodies with special damp, soapy cloths. The cloths have soap that does not have to be rinsed off. To clean their teeth, astronauts use a rinseless toothpaste that can be swallowed or spat out into a tissue.

Blood circulation is a problem in space because the heart does not have to pump blood up from the legs, as it does on Earth. This means astronauts often become dizzy when they return to solid ground.

SPACE SLEEPING

There is no such thing as lying down and sleeping in space. Instead, astronauts often attach their sleeping bags to a wall before climbing inside. On some space stations there are tiny bedrooms about the size of a refrigerator. Inside, a crewmember can store their sleeping bag and personal possessions in compartments, and roll a hatch over the top for privacy.

Most astronauts say eye masks and earplugs are essential to getting a good night's sleep on board a space station.

FIT FOR SPACE

One negative effect of weightlessness is that human muscles and bones become weaker. Earth's gravity pulls us down, which keeps our back and legs strong while they support our weight. To keep their muscles and bones healthy, astronauts have to exercise for at least 2.5 hours a day on treadmills and cycling machines.

TOILET TRAINING

Toilets in space are a bit like vacuum cleaners. Without suction, the human waste would float around the room. Astronauts urinate down a long tube, which can be attached tightly to the body. Solid waste also gets sucked away, but astronauts have to position themselves very carefully over a small toilet seat with a four-inch hole. A camera on the rim of the toilet helps them sit correctly. During spacewalks, astronauts wear a special diaper.

Solid human waste travels into a plastic bag, which is sealed and taken back to Earth with the other rubbish. Urine is often recycled into drinking water.

SPACE SHUTTLE

IN THE 1960s AND 1970s, COST WAS A MAJOR PROBLEM FOR SPACE EXPLORATION. SPACECRAFT WERE EXPENSIVE TO BUILD AND LAUNCH, AND EACH ONE COULD ONLY BE USED ONCE. Then, in 1981, NASA launched the world's first winged spaceplane: the Space Shuttle. The Shuttle could take off like a rocket and land like a plane. Because it was reusable, the Shuttle became a more affordable way of visiting space.

THREE COMPONENTS

The Space Transportation System, or Space Shuttle for short, was made up of three parts. The orbiter was the airplane-like section that carried the crew and cargo. Strapped to the orbiter were two booster rockets and a huge, rust-colored fuel tank. The booster rockets and fuel tank fell away after they launched the orbiter into space.

SHUTTLE DISASTERS

Between 1981 and 2011, five Space Shuttles were used for 135 successful missions. But there were also two tragic failures. In 1986, Space Shuttle Challenger exploded after it launched, killing all seven astronauts onboard. In 2003, disaster struck again when Space Shuttle Columbia disintegrated during its reentry to Earth. Once again, seven astronauts were killed.

Space Shuttle Challenger broke apart 73 seconds after liftoff when a seal failed and the leaked fuel exploded.

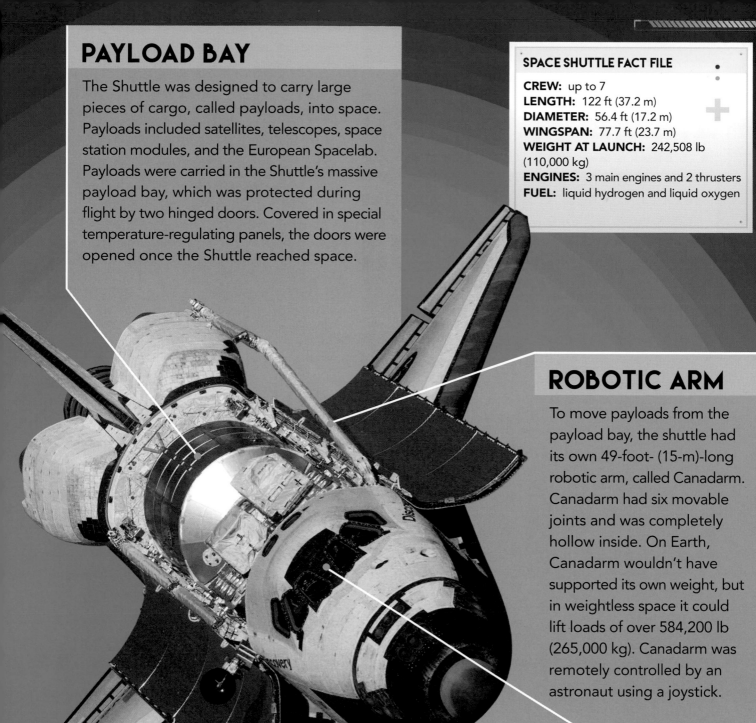

PAYLOAD BAY

The Shuttle was designed to carry large pieces of cargo, called payloads, into space. Payloads included satellites, telescopes, space station modules, and the European Spacelab. Payloads were carried in the Shuttle's massive payload bay, which was protected during flight by two hinged doors. Covered in special temperature-regulating panels, the doors were opened once the Shuttle reached space.

SPACE SHUTTLE FACT FILE

CREW: up to 7
LENGTH: 122 ft (37.2 m)
DIAMETER: 56.4 ft (17.2 m)
WINGSPAN: 77.7 ft (23.7 m)
WEIGHT AT LAUNCH: 242,508 lb (110,000 kg)
ENGINES: 3 main engines and 2 thrusters
FUEL: liquid hydrogen and liquid oxygen

ROBOTIC ARM

To move payloads from the payload bay, the shuttle had its own 49-foot- (15-m)-long robotic arm, called Canadarm. Canadarm had six movable joints and was completely hollow inside. On Earth, Canadarm wouldn't have supported its own weight, but in weightless space it could lift loads of over 584,200 lb (265,000 kg). Canadarm was remotely controlled by an astronaut using a joystick.

FLIGHT DECK

The Shuttle's flight deck was similar to that of an airplane, with two front seats for the mission commander and pilot, and a large instrument panel in front of them. Behind the flight deck was a mid-deck, where crewmembers worked, ate, and slept. The mid-deck contained sleep stations, a dining and work station, a kitchen galley, and a toilet and "personal hygiene station" for washing.

THE SHUTTLE: THERE AND BACK

THE COUNTDOWN TO A SHUTTLE LAUNCH BEGAN THREE DAYS BEFORE LIFTOFF. This allowed time for final safety checks and to fix any remaining issues. With 2.5 hours to go, the astronauts entered the Space Shuttle and took their seats. With one minute to go, the outside power was cut off and the Space Shuttle was ready to launch.

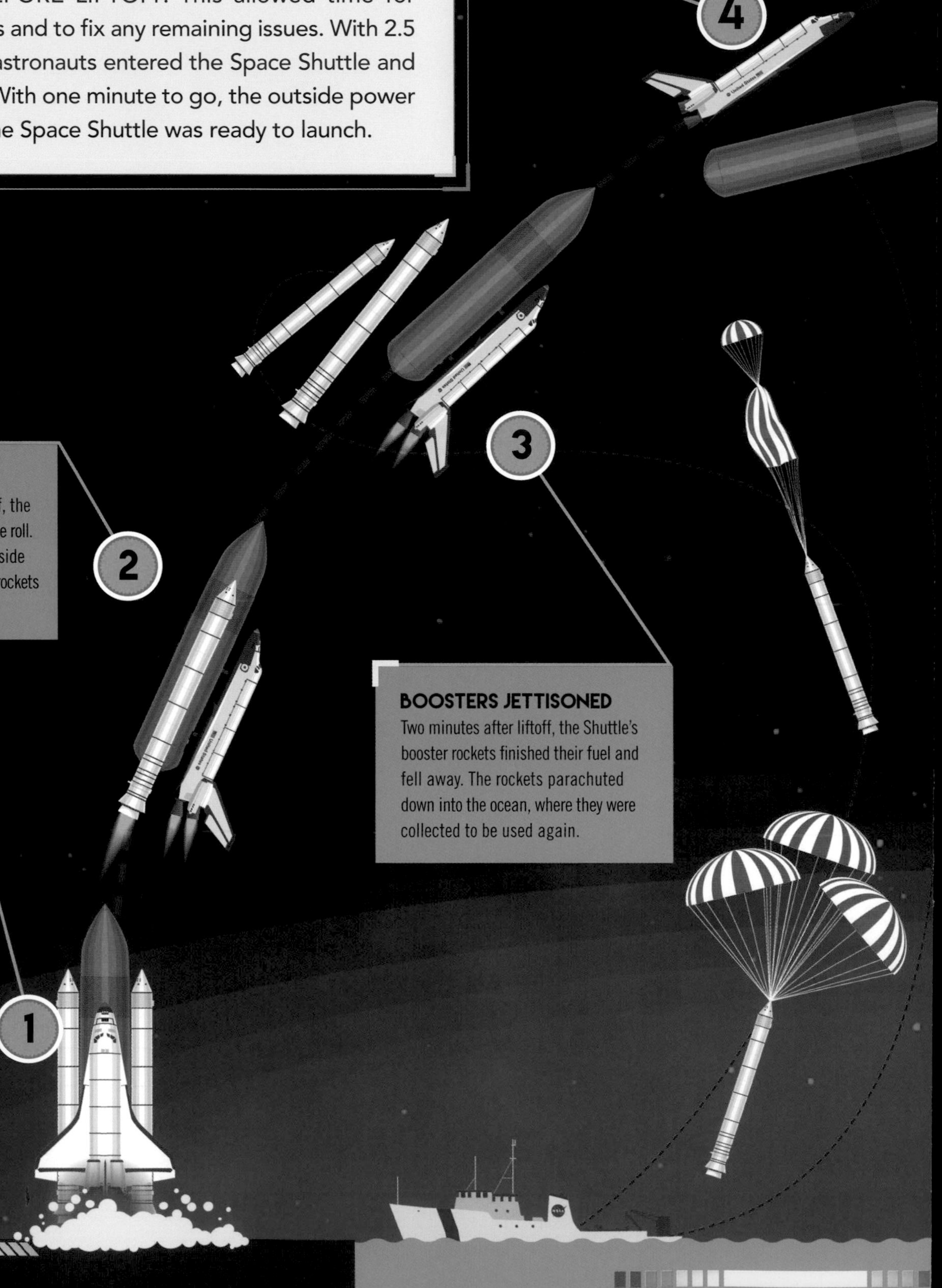

FUEL TANK FINISHED

Nine minutes after liftoff, the Shuttle's fuel tank fell back to Earth. This allowed the orbiter to roll around as if it was flying right-side up.

4

MID-AIR TURN

20 seconds after liftoff, the Shuttle did a 180-degree roll. This put the orbiter upside down, with the booster rockets and fuel tank on top.

2

3

BOOSTERS JETTISONED

Two minutes after liftoff, the Shuttle's booster rockets finished their fuel and fell away. The rockets parachuted down into the ocean, where they were collected to be used again.

LIFTOFF!

As the Shuttle's rocket booster fired, explosive bolts holding the Shuttle to the launch pad were fired. The Shuttle billowed smoke and steam from its engine nozzles and then lifted off.

1

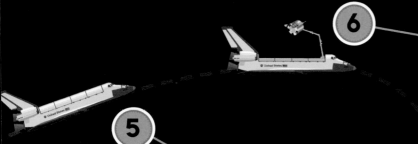

6

SPACE MISSION

The Shuttle stayed in space for the duration of its mission, which could be up to 30 days. When this was finished, the Shuttle prepared to reenter the Earth's atmosphere.

5

INTO ORBIT

Ten minutes after liftoff, the Shuttle's main engines fired to put it into a low orbit between 39 and 184 miles (64 and 296 km) above the Earth. About 30 minutes later, the Shuttle's two side engines fired to put it into a higher orbit.

7

SLOWING DOWN

For reentry to the atmosphere, the Shuttle fired its thrusters to slow it down and move out of Earth's orbit.

8

GLIDE TO GROUND

Once in the Earth's atmosphere, the Shuttle glided toward the landing site. Now it was moving over 20 times faster than a plane.

9

EARTH REENTRY

As it reentered Earth's atmosphere in a belly-up position, the Shuttle's bottom glowed orange-red from the friction with the air.

REPLAY HISTORY HERE!

NOSE UP

To land, the Shuttle lowered its wheels like an airplane, raised its nose, and touched down on the landing strip.

10

FAST LANDING

The Shuttle landed at a speed of about 220 mph (354 kmph). To slow down, it braked and released a 39-foot (12-m) drag chute from its tail. This helped bring it to a complete standstill.

11

FOR MANY YEARS, MIR HAD BEEN THE WORLD'S LARGEST SPACE STATION. But it was nothing compared to the International Space Station (ISS), a permanent satellite built by five different space agencies, that covers the area of a football field. First launched in 1998, the ISS is today made up of a Russian and a US Orbital Segment, which house crews from around the world for several months at a time.

ZVEZDA MODULE

Launched in 2000, the Zvezda Module contains the ISS's living quarters. About 538 sq ft (50 sq m) in size, the module contains sleeping compartments for two crewmembers at a time, a kitchen galley with a refrigerator, an exercise bike and treadmill, and a toilet. The module also contains an oxygen recycling system that takes waste water molecules and recycles them into oxygen and hydrogen. The oxygen is used to breathe and the hydrogen is vented into space.

ZARYA MODULE

The ISS's two Orbital Segments are made up of 16 modules: five from Russia, eight from America, two from Japan, and one from Europe. The Russian-built Zarya module was the first to be launched in 1998. It provided the ISS with electrical power during its early assembly and was built with three docking points. Today, it is mainly used for storage.

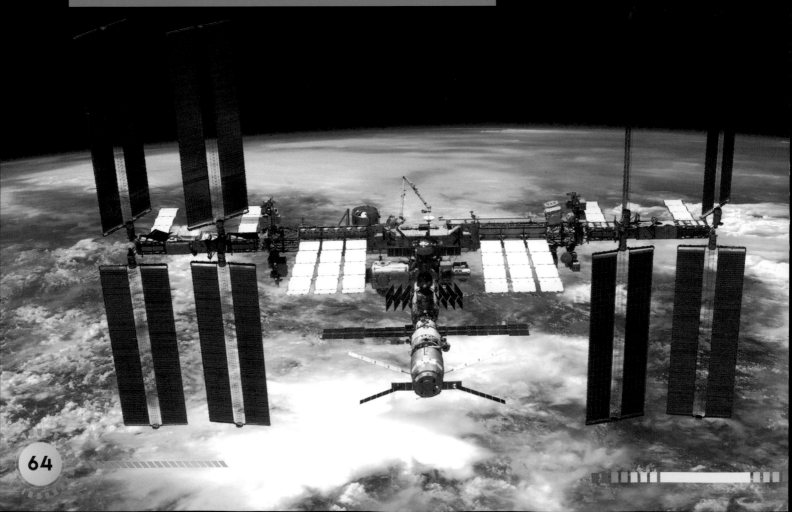

CANADARM2

The Canadarm2 is a 55-foot- (17-m)-long robotic arm that was used to assemble the ISS in space. Launched by Canada in 2001, the Canadarm2 is today a permanent fixture on the ISS. It is used to move equipment, undock cargo, and perform "cosmic catches": the capturing of unmanned spacecraft that travel from Earth. These spacecraft are used to bring all of the ISS's supplies, including food and water.

THE INTERNATIONAL SPACE STATION FACT FILE

CREW: up to 6
LENGTH: 239 ft (72.8 m)
DIAMETER: 356 ft (108.5 m)
NUMBER OF YEARS CONTINUOUSLY OCCUPIED: 17 (April 2018)
ORBITS PER DAY: 15

SEE IT IN 3D!

Look at these pages with the Space Race AR app on your smartphone or tablet to see a 3D model of the ISS in augmented reality.

COLUMBUS LABORATORY

The ISS has several laboratory modules, including the European Space Agency's Columbus module, which was launched aboard the Space Shuttle Atlantis in 2008. Some of the main experiments conducted onboard the ISS are on the impact of long stays in space on the human body. The loss of muscle mass and the weakening of bones are two of the negative effects of space.

SOLAR PANELS

To have electricity while flying 240 miles (386 km) above the Earth, the ISS uses a series of solar panels to convert sunlight energy into electricity. The panels are organized into wing-like arrays that stretch out from the space station. If placed together, these arrays would cover over 26,909 sq ft (2,500 sq m)—about half the area of an NFL football field. The arrays angle themselves to track the Sun and gain the greatest possible exposure to its rays.

SATELLITE EXPLORATION

A SATELLITE IS AN OBJECT THAT ORBITS A PLANET OR STAR. THE MOON IS A SATELLITE BECAUSE IT ORBITS THE EARTH. The Earth is a satellite because it orbits the Sun. Sputnik 1 was the Earth's first man-made satellite and since then over 6,600 satellites from 40 countries have been launched. Satellites are responsible for observing the Earth's environment, providing humans with communications, and observing the Universe beyond our planet.

COMMUNICATIONS

Satellites have changed the way humans communicate on Earth. Communications satellites pick up television, radio, telephone, and Internet signals and beam them back to other places on Earth. This gives us 24-hour-a-day access to information and each other. Today, there are about 2,000 communications satellites orbiting the Earth.

In 1962, Telstar became the first communications satellite to be launched. It was used to receive and then retransmit telephone and television signals.

EARTH WATCHERS

Weather and environmental satellites monitor conditions on Earth from above and send us information about what is going on. Weather satellites record data on everything from cloud cover and air temperature to wave height and wind speed. Environmental satellites provide important information about climate change on Earth, including shrinking ice fields, changes in vegetation, and the reduction of lakes and other freshwater.

Polar satellites travel in orbit around the Earth from north to south, while geostationary satellites orbit around the equator. But because many geostationary satellites are moving at the same speed as the Earth, they "sit" in one place and continuously view one region.

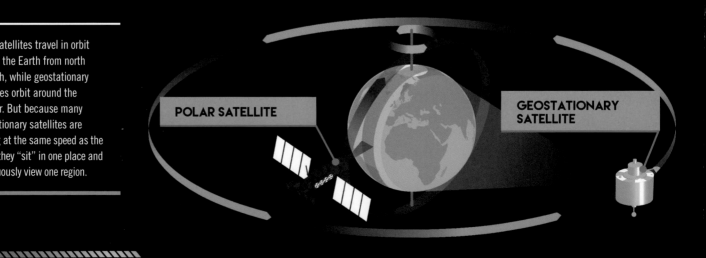

POLAR SATELLITE

GEOSTATIONARY SATELLITE

NAVIGATION

The US Navy launched the first satellite navigation system in the 1960s. It used a series of satellites working together to receive a signal from someone on Earth and then send another signal with the coordinates of exactly where they were. Today, similar systems are used in civilian life. We commonly access these positioning systems using our smartphones.

There are four global navigation satellite systems (GNSS) in use, including the United States' Global Positioning System (GPS), which many people access from their phones.

Overhead images of the Earth such as these were at one time only available to the military. They can now be easily accessed by civilians via the Internet.

SPY SATELLITES

Reconnaissance, or "spy," satellites are those used by governments for military purposes. Most commonly, these satellites take photos and record information about enemy territory. This information can include the details of troop movements, aircraft and missile launches, or chemical weapons installations. Because spy satellites are top secret, it is not known exactly how many each government has watching the Earth.

SPACE JUNK

It is estimated that of all the satellites launched, about 3,600 remain in orbit around our planet. The rest have either fallen back to Earth or burned up during reentry. Many hundreds of the remaining satellites, however, are defunct. These make up some of the man-made "space junk" that is currently in orbit around the planet. There are estimated to be tens of thousands of pieces of space junk, which range from flecks of paint to exhausted rocket stages and dead satellites.

A fleck of paint traveling in orbit can have the same impact as a 550 lb (250 kg) object traveling at 59 mph (96 kmph) on Earth. This puts other objects in orbit at risk.

5

PROBING THE PLANETS

HUMANS HAVE NOT VENTURED FAR IN THE EXPLORATION OF SPACE. Manned expeditions have only gone as far as our own moon. Unmanned robotic craft, however, have traveled much further. Dozens of space probes have been launched since the 1960s and they have explored all of the planets in our solar system. The information these probes have beamed back has shown that none of these worlds are hospitable to humans. But deep space probes hope to find new planets that we could one day inhabit.

SPACE PROBES

SPACE PROBES ARE A CLEVER WAY OF EXPLORING SPACE. They are cheaper than manned missions and can travel to worlds too dangerous for humans. However, once a probe has left the Earth's orbit, it is almost impossible to retrieve or repair it. Therefore probes have to be built with rugged and reliable instruments and be able to generate their own power. Probes that visit planets send back valuable information about the planet's gravity, its radiation levels, and its atmosphere and environment.

PIONEER TO JUPITER

The first probe to visit Jupiter and take photos of the planet was Pioneer 10, launched in 1972. Jupiter is the largest planet in the Solar System, located about 360 million miles (580 million km) from Earth. It took Pioneer 21 months to reach Jupiter and the probe had to fly through the hazardous Asteroid Belt to get there. As Pioneer passed Jupiter, it recorded data on the planet's radiation belts, magnetic field, and atmosphere. Pioneer then flew to the outer regions of the Solar System and last made contact at a distance of seven billion miles from Earth.

Over 1,300 Earths could fit into the massive gas planet Jupiter.

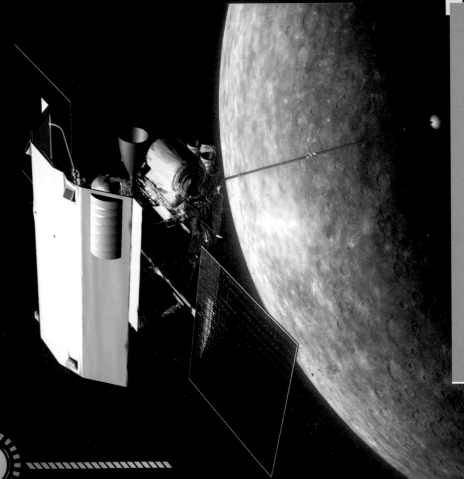

MARINER TO MERCURY

Launched in 1973, Mariner 10 was the first probe to visit both Venus and Mercury. After visiting Venus, Mariner 10 used the planet's gravitational pull to swing into a different orbit and fly onward to Mercury. Once there, it circled the planet three times and beamed back 2,800 images of the planet's surface. In 2011, a new probe called Messenger became the first to visit Mercury in over 30 years. It spent four years studying the planet's geology.

Mercury is the smallest planet in the Solar System, and the closest to the Sun. Before Mariner 10, no one had seen Mercury's surface because the Sun's solar glare obscured it.

MAGELLAN TO VENUS

Launched from the Space Shuttle Atlantis, the Magellan probe traveled to Venus in 1989 to map its surface. It did this with a large dish that bounced radar radio waves through Venus's thick, poisonous atmosphere and back to the probe. Magellan showed there was crater damage on Venus's surface, meaning some objects had been able to pass through its atmosphere.

The radar-mapping Magellan was the fifth NASA probe sent to Venus.

VOYAGERS INTO DEEP SPACE

Launched in 1977, Voyagers 1 and 2 are two of the most famous space probes. This is because their journey has lasted for over 40 years and Voyager 1 has traveled further into space than any man-made object. The probe recently reached interstellar space, which is the unknown area between our solar system and others. Voyager 1 amazed scientists in late 2017, when it fired its thrusters after 37 years of non-use. This meant the probe still had one or two years of life in it.

Voyagers 1 and 2 photographed Jupiter, Saturn, Neptune, and Uranus, before heading out of the Solar System.

REPLAY HISTORY HERE!

CASSINI-HUYGENS

THE CASSINI-HUYGENS TRIP TO SATURN IS CONSIDERED TO HAVE BEEN ONE OF THE MOST SUCCESSFUL PROBE MISSIONS TO DATE. One of the largest, heaviest, and most complicated unmanned spacecraft ever constructed, Cassini-Huygens was launched in 1997 and began its investigations of Saturn in 2004. As well as circling the planet, the spacecraft also launched the Huygens probe onto Saturn's moon, Titan. The Cassini-Huygens mission ended in 2017, when it burned up in Saturn's atmosphere.

BOOM

Cassini-Huygens had a 36-foot-(11-m)-long magnetometer boom (arm) that was used to record information about the magnetic fields around Saturn. This helped scientists understand Saturn's rings. The planet's rings are made up of billions of chunks of ice and rock that may be the remains of comets or moons. The rings stretch out for about 167,770 miles (270,000 km) but are very thin—only about 328 feet (100 m) thick.

MAGNETOMETER BOOM (ARM)

RADAR

Cassini-Huygens's onboard radar was used to bounce radio waves through the thick atmosphere of Titan and back to the spacecraft. This enabled it to build up a picture of the moon's surface that included mountains and canyons. As it circled Saturn, Cassini-Huygens discovered six new moons and evidence of water-ice on one of these moons, called Enceladus.

ANTENNA

Cassini-Huygens had one high-gain and two low-gain antennae to communicate with Earth. The high-gain antenna was the main communicator, but it was also used for scientific experiments and as an umbrella to shield the spacecraft's instruments. The low-gain antenna was a backup, in case of power failure or another emergency. It took between 68 and 84 minutes for Cassini-Huygens's radio signal to reach Earth.

POWER

Cassini-Huygens had one main engine and a backup engine. To provide electricity to its instruments, it used generators powered by a 70-lb (32-kg) block of plutonium. As plutonium radioactively decays, it delivers heat that can be converted to electricity. Plutonium had to be used because the probe was too far from the Sun for solar panels.

CASSINI-HUYGENS IN NUMBERS

4.84 billion miles
(7.8 billion km) traveled

453,048
photographs taken

162 flybys
of Saturn's moons

2.5 million commands
sent from Earth

294 orbits of
Saturn completed

6 new moons
discovered

ANTENNA

CASSINI SPACECRAFT FACT FILE

HEIGHT: 22 ft (6.7 m)

WIDTH: 13 ft (4 m)

WEIGHT AT LAUNCH: 12,831 lb (5,820 kg)

POWER: 3 Radioisotope Thermoelectric Generators (RTGs)

MAIN ENGINE AND SPARE

HUYGENS PROBE

HUYGENS PROBE

The Huygens probe was built with a hard shell to protect its instruments as it descended through the extreme temperatures of Titan's atmosphere. As it parachuted to the surface, Huygens took over 1,000 photographs of the moon as its instruments measured the atmosphere and beamed the information back to Cassini. Huygens landed on a shoreline created by methane, which probably played a similar role to water on Earth, eroding the rocky ground.

CURIOSITY IS A ROBOTIC CAR-SIZED ROVER SENT TO EXPLORE THE SURFACE OF MARS. Its aim is to investigate whether the planet could support human life. The longest and heaviest rover ever constructed, Curiosity was launched aboard a spacecraft called the Mars Science Laboratory (MSL) in 2011. But landing on Mars was to be a complicated task. Too heavy for parachutes, Curiosity would instead need to be lowered from its spacecraft using a system known as the "sky crane."

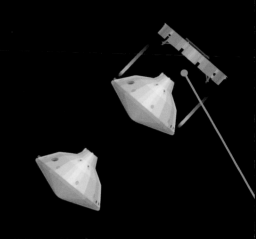

MARS IN SIGHT
On August 6, 2012, the cruise stage dropped away from the spacecraft 10 minutes before it hit Mars's atmosphere. The spacecraft was then traveling at about 18,507 mph.

HOT BOTTOM
As the spacecraft entered Mars's atmosphere, its heat shield reached a temperature of 3,812°F (2,100°C). Inside MSL it was only 50°F (10°C).

PARACHUTE OUT
At 7.2 miles above the surface of Mars, the spacecraft's parachute popped out, slowing it down to about 1,056 mph (1,700 kmph).

HEAT SHIELD OFF
Having done its job, the heat shield fell away at about 5.5 miles (8.8 km) above Mars's surface. The spacecraft's radar then began to calculate its altitude and landing speed.

FREE FALL
At 5,249 feet (1.6 km) above the surface, the shell protecting the descent stage dropped away. The descent stage then fired its retrorockets.

LANDING GEAR
With 62 feet (19 m) to go to the surface, the Curiosity rover was lowered from the descent module by 24-foot- (7.5-m-)long cables called the sky crane. The descent slowed down to about 16 mph (2.7 kmph).

WHEELS OUT
At 10.5 feet (3.5 m) above the surface, Curiosity's wheels came out for landing. The rover then touched down and the sky crane flew away so it wouldn't fall on top of the rover.

SEE IT IN 3D!

Look at these pages with the Space Race AR app
on your smartphone or tablet to see a 3D model
of the Curiosity rover in augmented reality.

CURIOSITY

Curiosity is about the size of a car, as high as a man,
and uses a 6-foot- (2-m)-long arm to collect soil and
rock samples. It also carries 17 cameras, a drill, and
a laser for vaporizing rock. It can analyze powered
samples of rock to look for evidence of microbes,
which indicate water. Excitingly, the rover did confirm
that there is water on Mars.

CURIOSITY ROVER FACT FILE

LENGTH: 9.8 ft (3 m)
WIDTH: 8.8 ft (2.7 m)
HEIGHT: 7.2 ft (2.2 m)
WEIGHT: 1,982 lb (899 kg)

NAVIGATION AND
PANORAMIC CAMERAS

NUCLEAR BATTERY

WEATHER SENSOR TO MEASURE
TEMPERATURE AND WIND SPEED

ROBOTIC ARM

SIX WHEELS

COMET RIDING

COMETS ARE MASSIVE CHUNKS OF ICE AND ROCK THAT MAY HOLD CLUES ABOUT THE BIRTH OF THE UNIVERSE. However, most comets stay in the outer reaches of the Solar System and rarely travel past the Earth. Before the space race, telescopes were the only way to study comets. But from the 1980s, unmanned probes were launched to fly past comets and collect data from them. Then, in 2004, a probe called Rosetta was launched to drop a lander onto a comet.

COMETS AND ASTEROIDS

Comets and asteroids are leftovers from a giant cloud of gas and dust that formed the solar system about 4.5 billion years ago. Asteroids are pieces of rock that measure between a few feet and a few miles across. Many are found in the Asteroid Belt between Mars and Jupiter. Comets form a tail as they travel toward the Sun. This causes their ice to melt, leaving a trail of vapor, gas, and dust behind.

Although most comets are less than 30 miles (48 km) across, their tails can stretch for many millions of miles (kilometers).

HALLEY'S COMET

Halley's Comet visits Earth every 75 years. This is because, like other comets, Halley's is in an elliptical orbit around the Sun. Scientists think comets may have preserved some of the original material that formed the Universe. To study this material, a probe called Giotto was launched to fly by and take photos of Halley's Comet when it visited in 1986.

Like the Earth, asteroids are typically in a round orbit around the Sun, but comets are usually in an elliptical orbit.

JUPITER'S ORBIT

SATURN'S ORBIT

URANUS'S ORBIT

NEPTUNE'S ORBIT

MARS'S ORBIT

EARTH'S ORBIT

COMET HALLEY'S POSITION AT GIVEN DATE

1985

1987

1983

1989

1977

1996

1948, 2024

Rosetta was a cube-shaped probe fitted with cameras and an aerial to study comet radio waves. The Philae lander was attached to it.

ROSETTA SPACECRAFT

In 2004, the European Space Agency (ESA) launched the Rosetta probe to study a comet called Comet 67P/Churyumov-Gerasimenko. After a ten-year journey, Rosetta reached the comet and went into orbit around it for 17 months. After taking photos, the probe launched its Philae lander to explore the comet and study rock samples. It was the first spacecraft to ever land on a comet.

ROSETTA PROBE

PHILAE LANDER

Philae was a small, box-shaped lander about 3 feet (1 m) across.

Even in its dark resting place, Philae's solar panels powered it back to life twice in 2015 and it was able to send information to the Rosetta probe.

PHILAE LANDER

On August 6, 2014, Rosetta's Philae lander touched down on Comet 67P/Churyumov-Gerasimenko. Almost immediately things went wrong. The lander was supposed to fire harpoons to stick into the comet's surface, but they did not work. Instead, Philae bounced on the surface and fell on its side in the shadow of a cliff. This meant the lander's solar panels could not collect sunlight, and its batteries ran out two days later.

BYE-BYE, PHILAE

After Philae was lost, the Rosetta probe continued orbiting Comet 67P/Churyumov-Gerasimenko. In 2016, it was decided to end the mission and crash-land Rosetta onto the comet. However, less than a month before its end, Rosetta took a surprise photo showing the Philae lander. Philae had fallen into a dark crack where sunlight could not reach. The discovery of Philae helped scientists understand the data it had sent back during its two operational days on the comet.

HUBBLE TELESCOPE

HUMANS HAVE USED TELESCOPES TO STUDY SPACE FOR CENTURIES. However, the light pollution caused by Earth's atmosphere always limited the view of a telescope on the ground. The answer was to place a telescope in space. In 1990, a bus-sized telescope called Hubble was delivered into the Earth's orbit aboard the Space Shuttle Discovery. Since then, Hubble's images of space have provided many insights into the wider Universe.

HUBBLE SPACE TELESCOPE FACT FILE

LENGTH: 43 ft (13.2 m)
DIAMETER: 39 ft (12 m) (with solar arrays)
WEIGHT: 24,250 lb (11,000 kg)
ORBIT: 1.8 ft (571 km) above Earth

BOUNCING MIRRORS

Hubble is equipped with a main 7.8-foot- (2.4-m) primary mirror, a smaller secondary mirror, and scientific instruments that study the Universe in infrared, visible, or ultraviolet light. These light sources are collected by Hubble's main mirror, reflected onto its smaller mirror, and then sent to its scientific instruments to analyze. The information is then beamed to Earth.

CUNNING CAMERA

Hubble's camera is its most important instrument. The camera can either take wide-field images of a stretch of space, or a high-resolution image of a single object such as a planet. Because it is in space, Hubble's camera can take an image with a resolution 10 times greater than any telescope on Earth. It can also detect objects that are 50 times fainter. This has resulted in many sharp images of parts of the Universe never before seen.

DATA DROP

Using its high-gain antenna, Hubble records and beams back around 120 gigabytes of information about the Universe every week. This information has been vital for astronomers. Among the telescope's images was the Hubble Deep Field, a photograph showing around 1,500 galaxies. The photograph has enabled astronomers to better understand how the Universe has evolved and how fast it is still expanding.

SPACE REPAIRS

After Hubble was successfully launched into space, it encountered a big problem. Although the telescope had cost over 1.4 billion dollars to build, it could not produce a sharp image. It was found that the telescope's main mirror was not correctly aligned. Instead, it was out of position by 1.3 mm. In 1993, Space Shuttle astronauts traveled to Hubble to fix the problem. Five more maintenance missions since have made sure the telescope stays in good shape.

Hubble can take images of distant planets and galaxies because it receives their ultraviolet light. This light cannot penetrate the Earth's atmosphere to reach telescopes there. As such, Hubble can take photos of young stars with discs around them, which will turn into solar systems such as our own.

6

INTO THE FUTURE

IN THE 1950s, THE DREAM OF SPACE EXPLORATION BECAME A REALITY FOR THE FIRST TIME. Scientists Sergei Korolev and Wernher von Braun turned rocket technology designed for terror and destruction into a way of sending men and machines into space. Today, there are plans for space tourism, bases on the Moon, and interstellar craft that will find habitable planets for humans to live on. It has been over 50 years since astronauts first set foot on the Moon, and colonizing faraway worlds is the modern dream of humankind. Perhaps traveling to different planets will soon be as common as the rockets that carry people to space stations above the Earth.

COMMERCIAL SPACEFLIGHT

DURING THE SPACE RACE, ONLY GOVERNMENTS HAD THE MONEY AND MEANS TO SEND PEOPLE INTO SPACE. The first space travelers were top Russian and American fighter pilots who trained for many months to become cosmonauts and astronauts. Soon, however, money may be all people need to experience weightlessness in space, travel in orbit around the Earth, or even visit the Moon. Experts say commercial spaceflights and space tourism will soon become commonplace.

FIRST SPACE TOURIST

In 2001, American businessman Dennis Tito became the first space tourist after paying to stay aboard the International Space Station for seven days. Although NASA was originally against the idea, it later saw the advantages of having people pay to visit space. After canceling its Space Shuttle program in 2011, NASA now pays Russia to send astronauts to the ISS aboard Soyuz spacecraft. By working with commercial spaceflight companies, NASA hopes to lower the price of sending astronauts to space and also raise some money for its own space programs.

Millionaire Dennis Tito became famous by being the first person to pay to fly into space. His experience cost a reported 20 million dollars.

The Dragon 2 spacecraft has room to transport seven astronauts and will launch aboard SpaceX's Falcon Heavy rocket.

SPACEX

In 2010, American company SpaceX sent supplies to the ISS aboard its unmanned Dragon spacecraft. It was the first time a company rather than a government had launched such a mission. Now SpaceX has a deal with NASA to send astronauts to the ISS aboard its new Dragon 2 spacecraft. The cost of a ticket aboard Dragon 2 would be about 58 million dollars, which is much cheaper than the 81 million dollars it costs for a seat aboard a Russian Soyuz. SpaceX says it is planning paid trips around the Moon in the future.

SpaceShipTwo has been in production since 2009, but suffered a major setback when one of its test spaceplanes crashed in the Mojave desert in 2014.

SPACESHIPTWO

British company Virgin has been offering tickets for its suborbital spaceplane SpaceShipTwo for several years. The spaceplane is designed to carry six passengers for a 180-minute flight, which will give them a few minutes in suborbital space. This means the spacecraft exits the Earth's atmosphere, but does not break out of the planet's orbit. SpaceShipTwo has sold over 600 tickets for about 250,000 dollars each and plans to launch its first passenger flight in 2019.

BLUE ORIGIN

Blue Origin is an American company with its eye on commercial spaceflight. Its New Shepard is a reusable vehicle made of a rocket and crew capsule that can take off and land in a vertical position. New Shepard is designed to take passengers on a suborbital flight. This means the spacecraft will launch to an altitude of about 62 miles (100 km) before slowing its ascent and landing back on Earth. Each flight would last about 10 minutes.

New Shepard would give high-paying customers the chance to experience a few minutes in space.

MISSION TO THE SUN

THE SUN IS THE LARGEST AND MOST IMPORTANT CELESTIAL OBJECT IN THE SOLAR SYSTEM. The Earth and seven other planets are all in orbit around the Sun. Without the Sun's heat and light, almost all life on Earth would die. Therefore, understanding the Sun has always been a top priority for scientists. In 2018, NASA launched the Parker Solar Probe to study how heat and energy travel away from the Sun. To do this, the probe will get closer to the Sun than any spacecraft has dared to go before.

THE SUN'S SOLAR WIND

The Sun constantly fires off energy particles in a "solar wind" that travels across the Solar System. Earth is protected from this wind by the planet's magnetic field. This is fortunate, because the solar wind travels at an incredible speed of about 1 million mph (1.6 million kmph). This makes the particles too fast for the Sun's gravity to hold on to. However, nobody knows what accelerates the solar wind to such a speed. The Solar Probe aims to find out.

Energy particles from the solar wind speed out past the Earth and into the far reaches of the Solar System.

TOO HOT TO HANDLE

The Parker Solar Probe will fly as close as 3.85 million miles (6.2 million km) to the Sun's surface. That sounds far away, but it's eight times closer than any spacecraft has gone before. Even at this distance, the probe needs a 4.5-inch-thick carbon heat shield to withstand temperatures of about 2,498°F (1,370°C). The Sun's outer layer is called the corona and is its hottest part. Temperatures in the corona range from 33–50 million °F (1–10 million °C). Scientists hope the probe will reveal why the corona is hotter than the Sun's core, which seems to go against the rules of physics.

The Sun's corona can be seen showing a solar flare, a sudden release of energy that looks like a bright flash.

SPACE WEATHER

The Sun is a massive ball of burning gases that provides heat and light for all life on Earth. However, its solar wind can shake Earth's magnetic field and interfere with its satellites. This is known as space weather, and the more scientists know about it, the more they can do to protect the many man-made satellites that humans now depend on. Space weather also dominates the environment in the outer Solar System. Understanding space weather will then help humanity's chances for long-distance space travel.

THERMAL PROTECTION SYSTEM

SOLAR ARRAY COOLING SYSTEM

SOLAR ARRAY WINGS

MAGNETOMETERS TO MEASURE MAGNETIC FIELDS

ANTENNA

The Sun is the biggest object in our solar system. If it were hollow, over one million Earths would fit inside the Sun. But our Sun is actually a relatively small star: a nearby star called Betelgeuse is about 700 times bigger and 14,000 times brighter.

THE PROBE

The Parker Solar Probe will take seven years to reach the Sun after first completing seven flybys of the planet Venus. Every time it gets near Venus, the probe's orbit will shrink, meaning that it gets closer and closer to the Sun. Altogether the probe will complete 24 orbits of our star. At its closest point to the Sun, the Parker Solar Probe's instruments will collect information about the solar wind. As this time, the probe will be traveling at 724,000 mph.

PARKER SOLAR PROBE FACT FILE

HEIGHT: 9.8 ft (3 m)
DIAMETER: 7.5 ft (2.3 m)
SOLAR ARRAY: 16.6 sq ft (1.55 m^2)
WEIGHT AT LAUNCH: 1,510 lb (685 kg)
ROCKET: Delta IV Heavy

WATCH THE SOLAR PROBE HERE!

MOON BASES

THE LAST TIME HUMANS WENT TO THE MOON WAS DURING THE APOLLO 17 MISSION IN 1972. The astronauts spent three days conducting experiments before blasting back to Earth. Since then, the great prize of the 1960s space race has been left alone. Today, however, the world is on the brink of a lunar return. Plans from several different governments include new robotic rovers to explore the surface, a space station that stays in lunar orbit, and a permanently occupied Moon village.

MOON VILLAGE

The Moon village is an idea for a lunar base being developed by the European Space Agency (ESA). It would be built out of several small domes using a 3-D printer and lunar soil. The soil would cover the domes and protect them from solar radiation from the Sun. The village would be situated at the lunar south pole, which gets year-round sunlight. The sunlight would power the village's solar panels and help plant life grow in lunar greenhouses. Scientists have discovered that carrots and tomatoes can grow in soil similar to that on the Moon.

The Moon village would be like an international lunar laboratory where crews could test whether humans could live permanently on the Moon.

WATER FOR LIFE

Humans cannot survive on another world without water. Space agencies were therefore excited by news in 2009 that India's Chandrayaan-1 probe had located water molecules on the Moon's surface. Water has also been discovered in tiny glass beads left over from lunar volcanic explosions. Many believe there are large reservoirs of water-ice trapped beneath the Moon's surface, with still more deposited in the Moon's craters. If collected, this water could be used for drinking and for watering plants, and it could also be split into its two chemical parts: oxygen and hydrogen. These could be used for breathing and also to create rocket fuel.

This infrared image from the Chandrayaan-1 probe shows that water is present in small quantities on the moon's surface.

MOON ROVING

During the space race, only the United States was able to visit the Moon. But today other countries are involved in Moon exploration. India's Chandrayaan-2 is a rover that will explore the lunar south pole and China's Chang'e-4 rover will become the first to visit the Moon's far side. Future missions will not only be about scientific research: many private companies are interested in mining the Moon's resources. These include water-ice, titanium, platinum, gold, iron, and the chemical Helium-3, which could provide power for nuclear reactors.

Governments and companies alike are excited to find and mine minerals and metals on the Moon.

BEYOND THE MOON

The space agencies of Russia, China, Japan, and Europe all have plans to put astronauts on the Moon in the coming decades. America, however, has announced it wants to go one step further. America's NASA has plans to place a radio telescope on the Moon and a space station in permanent orbit around it. The space station could act as a stopping-off point for missions on the way to a more difficult goal: Mars.

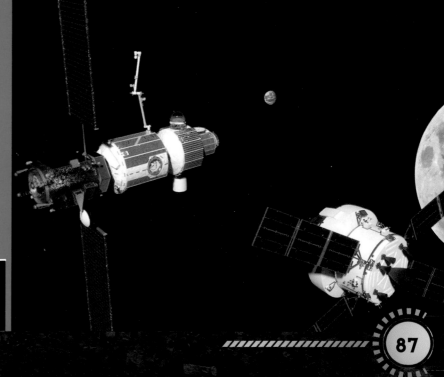

A lunar radio telescope would enable astrophysicists to study the period in the Universe's history when they believe the first stars were formed.

THE RACE TO MARS

A MANNED MISSION TO MARS IS A LONG-TERM GOAL FOR THE SPACE PROGRAMS OF SEVERAL COUNTRIES. One such mission could see astronauts travel to the red planet aboard NASA's Orion spacecraft. The Orion would be launched aboard a new megarocket called the Space Launch System (SLS) and would have room for four astronauts. It is unlikely the Orion mission would take place before 2030, and by then another country may beat America to it. The race to Mars could become the space race of the 21st century!

JOURNEY TIME TO MARS

The time taken to get to Mars depends partly on the route and partly on the size and type of spaceship used. At present it is thought that the shortest journey time between Earth and Mars would be nine months. Depending on how long the astronauts stayed on Mars, they could be away from Earth between 18 months and three years.

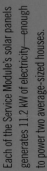

The Service Module's body is covered with an outer shell made to withstand the impact of high-speed micrometeoroid particles.

Each of the Service Module's solar panels generates 11.2 kW of electricity—enough to power two average-sized houses.

CREW MODULE

The Crew Module will transport four astronauts to and from the surface of Mars. It is reusable and, like the older and smaller Apollo capsules, has been designed to withstand the heat generated when traveling through an atmosphere to the surface of a planet.

THE SERVICE MODULE

The Service Module's cylindrical body is made from aluminum-lithium alloy and it has four solar panels that can be extended like wings to generate electricity from sunlight. It can supply power, oxygen, and life support systems for up to 21 days to support a crew of four in space.

ORION SPACECRAFT (ASTRONAUTS)

UPPER STAGE (LIQUID FUEL)

1. Earth departure
2. Mars arrival
3. Mars departure
4. Earth arrival

SPACE LAUNCH SYSTEM

To launch Orion into space, NASA is developing the most powerful rocket ever built: The Space Launch System (SLS). Taller than the Statue of Liberty, this expendable giant rocket generates more thrust than the Saturn V rockets that powered NASA's missions to the Moon.

SERVICE MODULE FACT FILE

LENGTH: 13 ft (4 m)   **DIAMETER:** 16 ft (5 m)
ENGINES: a main Space Shuttle OMS rocket engine, plus 8 secondary thrusters and 24 small maneuvering thrusters.
SOLAR ARRAY: 4 panels, each 23 ft (7 m) long
WATER: 240 liters in 4 water tanks
OXYGEN: 198 lb (90 kg) of compressed oxygen held in 3 tanks
FUEL: 19,841 lb (9,000 kg) in 4 x 2000 liter propellant tanks

SPACE LAUNCH SYSTEM FACT FILE

HEIGHT: 212 ft (64.6 m)
DIAMETER: 27 ft (8.4 m)
STAGES: 2
PAYLOAD: 143 tons (130 tonnes)
ENGINES: 5 liquid-fueled main engines, plus 2 detachable solid fuel boosters

**CORE STAGE
(LIQUID FUEL)**

**SOLID ROCKET
BOOSTER
(SOLID FUEL)**

Orion made its first test flight in December 2014. Successfully launched into orbit by a Delta IV rocket, the capsule returned safely to splashdown in the Pacific Ocean.

ENGINES

LIFE ON MARS

FOR DECADES, SCIENTISTS HAVE DREAMED OF BUILDING A HUMAN BASE ON MARS. Of all the planets, Mars is most like Earth: it has polar ice caps, an atmosphere, and even seasons. However, it remains a hostile planet for humans. Mars's surface is dusty and desert-like, its thin atmosphere is made mainly of carbon dioxide, and temperatures on the surface can drop to −148°F (−100°C). Despite this, several planned missions to Mars in 2020 all have the same aim: to investigate the possibility of humans living there.

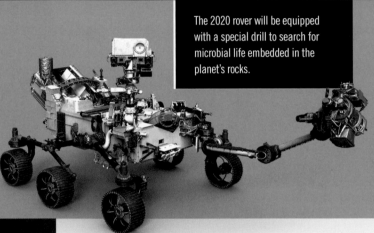

The 2020 rover will be equipped with a special drill to search for microbial life embedded in the planet's rocks.

NASA ROVER

The Mars 2020 rover mission is part of NASA's long-term exploration of the red planet. The rover's mission will be to test technologies that can be used for the first manned mission. These include a machine that produces oxygen from Mars's carbon-dioxide atmosphere. It will also search for resources, such as water, that could be mined during the first human visit.

EUROPEAN AND RUSSIAN ROVER

ExoMars is a joint European and Russian mission that will deliver a rover to Mars in 2020. The rover will land at a site scientists believe may contain signs of life on the planet. By digging to a depth of 6 feet (2 m), the rover aims to find evidence of plant or simple animal life that may have existed in Mars's past. This would prove it is possible for life to exist on the planet.

ExoMars is timed for an August 2020 launch. This is when the orbits of Mars and the Earth are at the shortest distance away from each other, at 33.8 million miles (54.5 million km).

HOPE MARS MISSION

The Hope Mars Mission is a car-sized probe being sent to Mars in 2020 by the United Arab Emirates. It will be the first mission to Mars by a Muslim country. After being launched, the probe will take 200 days to reach Mars and spend two years orbiting the planet. During this period, it will study the Martian atmosphere for traces of water and oxygen and beam the results back to Earth.

EMIRATES MARS MISSION

مشروع الإمارات لاستكشاف المريخ

مسبار
الأمل
HOPE

This ambitious landing will be the first of its kind attempted on Mars.

The Hope Mars Mission will study the possibility of growing date palms and lettuce in the Martian soil.

CHINA'S MARS MISSION

China is also planning a Mars mission in 2020. The mission will consist of a probe that will orbit the planet and a lander that will descend to the surface. To land safely, the lander will use a parachute, a gasbag, and reverse-thrust engines. Once on the ground, a six-wheeled rover will exit the lander and explore. It will also use a ground-penetrating radar to see what is below the surface. After three months, the rover's batteries are expected to be exhausted and the mission will focus on the probe's findings from orbit.

MARSBEES

To explore Mars by air, NASA is investigating the development of a swarm of tiny flying robots called Marsbees. Each robot would be about the size of a bumblebee and be fitted with sensors and wireless communication systems. The robots would fly around the planet recording information and feeding it back to a Mars rover, which would also be used as a charging point.

The "marsbees" could work together as a swarm to record data and map Mars.

IN THE SHORT STORY OF SPACE EXPLORATION, HUMANS HAVE MADE MANY AMAZING BREAKTHROUGHS. But we have still not traveled far. Beyond the Moon, Mars and the planets of the Solar System is the vast unknown of space. Our own Sun is only one of billions of stars in the Milky Way Galaxy; there are at least 100 billion galaxies in the Universe. The size of the Universe is almost impossible to imagine. Within this expanse, it is likely there are other planets like Earth, and other forms of life.

Scientists hope that TESS will find a "Goldilocks planet": one that is not too hot or too cold, but the perfect distance from its sun to support life, like the Earth.

LOOKING FOR EARTHS

The Transiting Exoplanet Survey Satellite (TESS) is a space telescope that will search for planets outside our solar system that could support life. After being launched into Earth's orbit, TESS will identify over 20,000 exoplanets—planets that orbit a star. To do this, TESS will survey the entire sky and break it up into 26 sectors. Then each sector will be examined in more detail.

SEARCHING FOR ALIENS

Are there aliens living somewhere out in the Universe? Many astronomers agree it is likely there are. But no one can agree on what form alien life might take. The Search for Extraterrestrial Intelligence (SETI) center is looking for alien life. Part of its work is using powerful radio telescopes to scan for radio signals sent by intelligent beings. The hope is that alien beings as developed as humans are also searching for life on different worlds.

China's Five hundred-meter Aperture Spherical Telescope (FAST) is one of the largest radio telescopes in the world. The size of five NFL football fields, the telescope contains 4,450 panels and is searching for alien communication signals.

SENDING MESSAGES

In 2017, an organization called Messaging Extraterrestrial Intelligence (METI) sent a radio message to two exoplanets circling a star called GJ 273. The message contained information about human life. GJ 273 is 12 light years away, so a response from any aliens living on the planets would take around 25 years to return to Earth. The METI message is not the first to be sent to potential aliens. In 1974, a radio message was sent from the Arecibo radio telescope towards the M13 star cluster, which is around 21,000 light years away. A response will take nearly 50,000 years to reach the Earth.

Famous cosmologist Stephen Hawking once warned that finding an advanced alien civilization could be dangerous, as the aliens might want to take over the Earth and destroy humanity.

PROBING THE BOUNDARIES

Deep space probes that fly out of our own solar system and toward different stars are one possible way of making contact with alien life. The most famous deep space probe is Voyager 1, launched by NASA in 1977 to explore the outer planets in our solar system. After that, however, it kept going. It has now traveled further than any other spacecraft and is currently 13 billion miles (21 billion km) from Earth. In case Voyager 1 ever met any aliens, a gold record explaining life on Earth was included onboard. The record contains sounds such as those made by weather and animals, and greetings in 55 languages. Imagine who—or what—might find it one day!

Voyager's gold record contains images showing life on Earth, including diagrams of the Earth and human beings. There are also instructions on how to play the record.

LOOK INTO THE FUTURE HERE!

INDEX